TARGETING TRANSFORMATION

EVERY PERSON, EVERY DAY, EVERY PLACE, EVERY TIME

Ray D. Ellis

WESTBOW
PRESS®
A DIVISION OF THOMAS NELSON
& ZONDERVAN

Scripture quotations marked (NIV) are taken from the Holy Bible, New International Version®, NIV®. Copyright © 1973, 1978, 1984, 2011 by Biblica, Inc.™ Used by permission of Zondervan. All rights reserved worldwide. www.zondervan.com The "NIV" and "New International Version" are trademarks registered in the United States Patent and Trademark Office by Biblica, Inc.™

Scripture quotations are taken from the Holy Bible, New Living Translation, copyright ©1996, 2004, 2007, 2013, 2015 by Tyndale House Foundation. Used by permission of Tyndale House Publishers, Inc., Carol Stream, Illinois 60188. All rights reserved.

Scripture quotations marked (MSG) in this publication are taken from The Message. Copyright © by Eugene H. Peterson 1993, 1994, 1995, 1996, 2000, 2001, 2002. Used by permission of NavPress Publishing Group.

Scripture quotations marked (KJV) are taken from the King James Version.

WestBow Press books may be ordered through booksellers or by contacting:

WestBow Press
A Division of Thomas Nelson & Zondervan
1663 Liberty Drive
Bloomington, IN 47403
www.westbowpress.com
1 (866) 928-1240

Because of the dynamic nature of the Internet, any web addresses or links contained in this book may have changed since publication and may no longer be valid. The views expressed in this work are solely those of the author and do not necessarily reflect the views of the publisher, and the publisher hereby disclaims any responsibility for them.

Any people depicted in stock imagery provided by Thinkstock are models, and such images are being used for illustrative purposes only.
Certain stock imagery © Thinkstock.

ISBN: 978-1-5127-6638-7 (sc)
ISBN: 978-1-5127-6639-4 (hc)
ISBN: 978-1-5127-6637-0 (e)

Library of Congress Control Number: 2016919618

Print information available on the last page.

WestBow Press rev. date: 01/04/2017

Dedicated to my wife, Dewenia:

No one deserves my thanks more than you. You have been
my encourager and my strength to stay the course in this work
and in this life. We have mutually agreed to walk through this
life together in every stage of deep water or gentle walks along
the quiet shore—whichever place the Lord has in mind for us on
any given day. I would not want to share this journey with anyone
else. Thank you!

Love you,
Ray

CONTENTS

Part 1—Setting the Sights

Part 2—Narrowing the Target

Part 3—Zeroing in on the Target

ACKNOWLEDGMENTS

There have been a few times in my life that have challenged me way beyond my capabilities. Those times that required jumping off a cliff into deep waters where I had never been before. Writing this book has certainly been one of those.

I never would have accomplished the task without my friend Christian Penrod. Christian encouraged me to write the book in the first place. He did not accept my first draft, but challenged me at every step along the way—sometimes with gentleness. He guided me in navigating the deep waters when I would have drowned in the process without him. Thank you!

I have been encouraged by my group of friends who meet Thursdays at noon. They understand transformation and continue to motivate me in this journey. They have allowed me to be a part of the group—to see their love of people, and their desire to help each person come closer to Christ. Thank you!

I relied greatly on my grandson, Dakota Ellis, who used his newly earned English degree from Taylor University to clarify this work. He took my floundering at writing and brought the ideas into complete sentences with correct spelling and punctuation. Thank you!

I would not have completed the book you are now holding without the skills of Amanda Bratschie. She enthusiastically shared her editing expertise to rearrange and improve my ideas.

Amanda also did the graph and map you will see in these pages. She is a professional in every way and without her direction and input I would still be struggling to finish this process. Thank you!

Finally, I have appreciated the service that WestBow Press provided. They are a group of professional people who are willing to come alongside a beginner like me to make this dream a reality. They offered guidance to me in every step of this process, from the introduction, through the editing, book cover, printing, distribution and every stroke of the pen in the middle. Thank you!

May God receive the glory!

Ray

DIRECTION OF FOCUS

Romans 12:2

And be not conformed to this world: but be ye transformed by the renewing of your mind, that ye may prove what is that good, and acceptable, and perfect will of God (KJV).

Do not conform any longer to the pattern of this world, but be transformed by the renewing of your mind. Then you will be able to test and approve what God's will is – his good, pleasing and perfect will (NIV).

Don't copy the behavior and customs of this world, but let God transform you into a new person by changing the way you think. Then you will know what God wants you to do, and you will know how good and pleasing and perfect his will really is (NLT).

Don't become so well-adjusted to your culture that you fit into it without even thinking. Instead, fix your attention on God. You'll be changed from the inside out. Readily recognize what he wants from you, and quickly respond to it. Unlike the culture around you, always dragging you down to its level of immaturity, God brings the best out of you, develops well-formed maturity in you (MSG).

PART 1

Setting the Sights

Then Jesus said this prayer: "O Father, Lord of heaven and earth, thank you for hiding the truth from those who think themselves so wise and cleaver. Yes, Father, it pleased you to do it this way!" (Matthew 11:25-26 NLT)

PART I

CHAPTER 1

A Rocky Beginning

Our lives are a voyage of discovery.
—John Stott, *Basic Christianity*

When I was eight years old, my grandmother died. Her name was Grace, and her loss rocked our family. I never knew my grandfather could feel so much pain and shed so many tears. At the funeral, he tried to take Grace's body out of the casket; he didn't want to let her go. Grandpa spent the next part of his life in pain and loneliness that was quietly shared with all those around him.

Grace was a strong, stout woman and more or less the matriarch of our clan. She was lovingly stern in all situations, and she knew very well how to have her voice heard and followed. Something about her strong German heritage and independent upbringing gave her a powerful personality. Her kids and their families were expected to be present at her house on Christmas, Easter, Thanksgiving, and any other time she wanted the family together, which was often. My dad was her youngest, and since we lived on a farm just down the road, I was at my grandparents' house almost every day.

When Grace left, things changed. We started going to church. I'm not sure that we started going to church just because Grandma died, but from my point of view, there was a strong connection. We'd never talked about heaven or hell much at home before then, but now, in church, we heard the concepts preached about every Sunday. I didn't like church much.

However, I liked the preacher. I liked that he would come to our farm and hunt. My dad said that was unusual for preachers. It was one thing to watch the preacher in coat and tie yell, pound the pulpit, and sweat on Sunday morning. Oh, did he sweat. I had never heard anyone talk about God the way he did. His words stabbed deep into my mind with images of God as a gray-haired, bearded old man, staring sternly down from his lofty position and pointing his finger at little boys like me. I believe this view of an old, gray dictator took the place of Grace. She was sorely missed. However, my salvation came on the Saturdays that the preacher brought his twelve-gauge shotgun and joined the other men on fox drives through the fields and woods in our county. That seemed to make the man more real and God less harsh.

But there was more about church I didn't like. Judging people by what they had or didn't have, by the way they lived, by the way they talked, or by the amount of money they seemed to have was not a way of life at our house during the week. But it seemed to be so on Sunday at the Lord's house. It was bad enough that I had to wear those special "dress slacks" and "Sunday shoes" with a nice, white shirt and sometimes even a tie. I preferred my normal blue jeans, work boots, and T-shirt, but my mom insisted. The orders on Sunday were, "Do not get these clothes dirty." I also had to sit still for what seemed like hours on end. By the time I reached my teen years, my tight-legged slacks and bright-colored shirts often received disapproving looks from older ladies and gentlemen in the congregation. By that time, I didn't much care. But then there was Gary.

Gary was my friend in school. He lived next to the railroad

tracks in town, and he came to church just to see what went on there; he had never been before. I'm not sure that I ever really asked him to attend, but it was nice to have him. The first week he came, before class, my Sunday school teacher asked Gary his name and where he lived. Gary told him, and the teacher shook his head and said, "Oh, you're from that bunch" and began teaching the class. I don't think the teacher ever looked at Gary again. That ticked me off. Where was God's grace in that teacher's life? It didn't take Gary and me many weeks to learn that we could leave the church building after Sunday school and walk around town, which was a lot more fun than listening to the new preacher pound the air and throw his Bible at us. Instead, Gary took me to his house on Sunday morning; that's how I met his family. It was clear from that day that his family lived a different lifestyle than mine. However, they welcomed me into their home and asked me about my family, my parents, school, and life on the farm. When I answered, they listened. I felt wanted, and I liked it. Gary did not attend church for long after that, and neither did I.

I doubt it's fair to compare the welcome Gary received in church with the one I received in his home. But from my perspective, as I look back through the years and compare the congregation of my childhood to the many church families I have had the privilege of being with through the years since, these two seem to bring the key elements of transformation into an understanding that I can discuss and share. Why did the leaders of our first church not want Gary there? What had he done wrong? Gary experienced a feeling of not being wanted, not being cared about, and mostly being invisible—except for the frowns and unfriendly looks of disapproval.

Because of these interactions, my dad and I had to talk about church, or at least my attendance in it. I made it clear I was not going back, and my dad made it clear I needed to be there.

He also informed me that he knew I had been skipping out of church for many weeks and that lying to him was not making our discussion any better. Dad knew a lot. He cared about me, and saying things like, "Bad company corrupts good behavior" were strong arguments in his favor. My dad did, after all, inherit a lot of strength and powerful qualities from his mother, but so did I. Dr. James Dobson might have labeled me a "strong-willed child." At that time, however, my dad was more in tune with the term "rebellious teenager." My dad reminded me that at nine years of age, I had walked down the aisle of this same church building and accepted Jesus as my Savior. I was baptized in the church for the forgiveness of my sins. "What happened to that boy?" he asked. "I don't know," was my only reply.

When you don't like church, you will find some reason to stop going. Blaming the people inside the building where you worship is often good enough. It was easy for me to point at the people inside the building on Sunday and how differently I saw them acting during the week. I spoke clearly about the man who had the oak leaf lapel pin on his suit jacket, a reward for one year of perfect Sunday school attendance. Under that oak leaf, he had several banners, meaning it had been years since he had missed a week at church. I said to my dad, "But we know he doesn't live the way he should the other six days of the week."

My dad's reply was swift. "No matter; he is not you." After that, I stopped going.

Today, my argument would be much different. Back then, I just knew something was not right. Even then, I knew that heaven and hell were not the only reasons to take a bath on Saturday night, put on dress clothes, and carry your Bible into a building on Sunday. There had to be more. Did those people at church care about me? Did they seek me during the week and talk to me then, in the act of living real life? Was my friend Gary feeling the same things I was, and did neither of us know how to express our individual voids? Why did I persist in judging the hypocrisy of others when, at the same time, it made me mad that they were so harshly judging me and my friend? Were they trying to speak the love of Jesus into my life, and I wasn't listening? Or were they trying to get me to be "good" like them, to perform and live two lives like them, therefore meeting their group standards so I could fit in and be accepted?

If the church had cared about Gary in a different way, would their love and care have kept him out of prison a few years later? Or is it possible that the part I learned in church helped me stay out of that adjoining cell? Maybe it was the discussion with my dad—having not fully sunk in until later—that made the difference for me. Or maybe the major factor was the love I knew at home that Gary might have been missing. I don't have all the answers, even today, but I have been searching for them. During that time of my life, I really missed Grace, both the physical person I had known and the spiritual one I had yet to learn about. I believe there needed to be a revolution in my heart and in the hearts of many folks who could speak into my life.

Several years later, after my wife and I married and had two sons, we decided it was time for us to find a church. We had not been attending anywhere, but we wanted good things for our family. We wanted our children to learn, think, and make their own decisions. So based on my earlier experiences, we did not want to go back to the church where I was raised; we wanted a church of our own.

There was a small church down the road from us, but friends of ours had family who attended, and they said, "You won't like that church." We went there once, but they must have been right because we never went back. There was another church a little farther away, and we began attending that one. During our second week there, we were asked to help with the children's Sunday school. We declined. Almost every week we were asked to help in some way or another. It was particularly troubling to me that at the end of the worship service, the preacher would look over the congregation and call on one of the men to have the closing prayer. My fear heightened greatly when I realized he did not ask these men before he called on them, meaning he might call on me. At the end of each service, I started keeping my head down, looking closely at the floor, hoping that if the preacher and I did not make eye contact then he would not call my name. We soon stopped attending. But the church did not stop asking. Members of that congregation would stop by on their way home from worship and knock on our front door. We didn't answer.

One day, an elderly man, and a leader of that church, stopped by while I was outside working. He said the preacher had been accused of some wrongdoing and had been fired. The preacher told this man that if he was "forced out," he would take more than half of the congregation with him, causing the church to fold. The elderly man said, "Please come this Sunday and help us. Just like if I had a flat tire on the road, you would certainly stop and help me. We need you this Sunday." We went that one Sunday, for that one man, but we never went back.

A few years later, we moved to a farm away from that community. Very few people in our new location knew us, but some of our new neighbors stopped and invited us to the church they belonged to. Again, we wanted to find a good church and decided to visit some of the local churches. At one church we immediately felt welcomed. People talked to us, encouraged us, and made us feel like a part of the congregation. My wife accepted Christ in that church and we were soon asked to help in many ministries and church committees. This time, it felt good to say yes.

But something kept troubling me. There was much work to do with the farming business, we had kids to raise, and we were putting money in the offering plate that we could be using on other things. Was this "church" thing real? Was this the place that God intended for us, and if it was, why were there so many problems within the congregation? Since my earlier experiences of church still lingered in my mind, why were there so many people in this new congregation questioning certain others who came to the worship service?

My family had been accepted, so why wasn't everyone being accepted? Why was there a dress code of suit and tie if you were serving communion? We were promoting Jesus as Savior and "doing Bible things in Bible ways," but why were we so tied to an endless list of rules and literally, forty pages of bylaws? It seemed to me that we were more interested in making people perform like us than we were in helping them be like Jesus. I was challenged in my work as a church volunteer because I began to see the struggles of church leadership. I saw full-time ministers, pastors, and paid staff who did not seem to have the same goals as their fellow workers, and the goals they did have were not aligned with the goals of the church leadership or other congregation members. There always seemed to be a battle of the will versus the want within the church family.

The church would talk the talk. "Jesus is the answer," we would say out loud. Those words always sounded good, but the words were most often just hot air whistling over our heads. There was nothing real or concrete that bonded us together. There was no lasting justification to continue the labor of bringing folks to Christ—no real plan to train, retain, or help the new Christians grow. We had good programs, but often "my program" conflicted with "their program," or the budget did not produce enough income to fund both opportunities, as well as all the others that were on the table, so one needed to be cut. We always said the cut was just for the season, because maybe we would use it in the future. Maybe.

It was that very congregation who encouraged me to train for and enter into the ministry. This came about because our preaching minister lost his voice. There were three times while he was preaching on Sunday mornings that his voice involuntarily stopped and he was not able to continue with the message. This was traumatic for a man who was skilled and loved to preach; however, it became clear to the church leadership, and to our preacher, that God was moving his life in another direction. As this man transitioned to a new location and ministry, our elders allowed me to serve as our interim minister. This position lasted about four months, and it became my introduction to full-time ministry.

As a result, I enrolled in Bible college at forty-six years of age, and in my head, I carried a list of questions—questions that had been unanswered in my years of serving as a church elder, deacon, and missions chairman. These questions were mostly centered on theology in one form or another, as well as some biblical clarity questions, and the big one: What does God really want from me? I was not the guy who was prone to hold up his hand in class and draw attention to himself by asking these questions out loud. After all, most of the students were twenty-plus years younger, and I didn't want to appear to be the old guy who had no clue. I would merely listen in each class and to each conversation on campus, and if an area of concern was verbalized, I paid special attention. I wanted to learn the good news, and I did.

But I also learned a troubling lesson. As I walked the halls, sat in the classrooms, and listened to people at lunch, I learned that so many other students were struggling with the same things I had struggled with in my local church. I had many conversations with good men and women, all serving churches across the country, and we were all engaged in the same battles. They would openly verbalize the lack of uniformity of purpose within their congregations. These students were trying their best to learn and to serve, yet so much of their time and energy was consumed with the political tension of navigating the day-to-day battles of self-will and personal motivation that existed between the church staff and church leadership. They understood that Jesus was still the answer, but He did not always seem to be the most prevalent commitment. This knowledge, these comments, and this dysfunction troubled me greatly. I had been naïve enough to think that the struggles I had experienced represented only a small part of the churches throughout the country. I learned then and there that this type of dysfunction is widespread and damaging to too many good congregations and Christian churches, but I had no idea what to do about it.

CHAPTER 2

Clarifying the Journey

We encounter God in the ordinariness of life: not in
the search for spiritual highs and
extraordinary mystical experiences but in our simple
presence in life.
—Brennan Manning, *The Rabbi's Heartbeat*

Serving as a full-time minister while, at the same time, attending college and graduate school was a rewarding challenge for me. During the time I spent in the classroom, I had the privilege of having many conversations with some very dedicated individuals who wanted to serve the Lord in many different ways; their education was just a part of that duty. Then, living life within the local church, I worked with individuals whose dedication and desire to serve the Lord was solid and real, who were serving through the church as volunteers or church staff. Yet both of these groups struggled to find clear, cohesive direction or purpose. I continued to listen and learn, but when I asked any questions about a single purpose, or if I initiated programs to bring individuals together, it often created more problems than it solved.

Then, after some six years of being in a classroom while also serving as a full-time minister, I was blessed with an encounter that changed my thinking and set me on the path to the sought-after answer to my questions. Why is there so much dysfunction in the church, and why does the church not agree on a single purpose? This one encounter hit me like a lightning bolt had struck out of a clear blue sky.

While I was studying for a master's degree in pastoral counseling, our professor, Dr. Dale Bertram, introduced our class to Mike Rankin, a guest speaker. We were only told that Mike had served for several years as a Catholic priest and was now devoting his full energy to counseling. At that time, Mike was running his own counseling practice in Louisville, and Dr. Bertram thought that we could learn a great deal from Mike's counseling style and process. He was right.

When Mike came to the front of the class, he started by asking one question. "What is the one goal you have for each and every client that enters your counseling office? The one goal that you maintain for each and every client, each and every day, which is the same goal for each and every person, each and every session?" We gave him many answers. All were wrong.

Then he said, "Let's bring the answer down to one word." We still could not get it. Finally, he gave us the answer: transformation. He went on to clarify. "You should make it your goal to listen to your clients for the purpose of understanding where they are on their spiritual journey and then help them get one step closer to God. You should stay determined to help them on their road of transformation, or in other words, being like Christ—each and every person, each and every time, each and every day. If you do this, your counseling will be successful."

I remember little about the rest of that class. Mike had set my mind in motion. I was remembering so many people who had walked through my life consumed by some struggle that had gone unresolved. Was this the answer that would help them? Was this the direction I had been longing for? I didn't sleep well that night. My mind kept churning this idea over and over. The words, "every person, every time, every day" continued to roll and bang around in my brain. The idea was revolutionary to me! What if this was the common ground that my fellow students and I had been looking for? What if my friend Gary had encountered a group of people in the local church who were totally focused on helping him be like Christ, and not so focused on who he wasn't at the time, or who his parents and family were? What if that congregation had understood personal transformation and lived that idea seven days a week? What if all congregations set that in their mind, preached that from their pulpits, and shared that in their day-to-day living? What would, or could, the church become by agreeing to the common goal of helping each person along his or her road of transformation?

It took many years of consideration, prayer, and personal debate, but that day in class set my mind on the belief—and the journey—that we could all have one common goal—not just in counseling sessions, not just inside the church building or the worship services, or even the life groups and Bible studies, but in all of life. My next struggle was how to do this in real, everyday life. How? How could I possibly begin to take the basic concept that Mike had so directly instilled in my mind and share it with others? How would other people receive this information? After all, we're all in different places of our spiritual journey. Each person's journey of life and daily experiences are different. However, transformation—and helping others with their transformation—could, at least in my mind, be the key.

To be successful with any steps forward, I had to fully understand and face the fact that we all study different things, in different ways, at different times in our lives. Some people like to study the arts, science, math, the latest fashion trends, or the coolest video games. Some like to look carefully at practical application, while others prefer theory and reason. Some like to have endless conversation about topics, while others just want to boil down the rhetoric into a few needed sentences and get to the point. Therefore, as we proceed through the years, life can alter our view about what is important. What we need, want, or must learn today may be totally different than what we felt was important in the past. As well, the past or present may have no bearing on what we will be drawn to in the future.

For me, working toward a pastoral counseling degree required studying many psychological theories. We had to understand the basic idea and language behind things like behavior theory, cognitive theory, attachment theory, and many others. My fellow students and I may or may not have felt a genuine interest, or been drawn to these ideas, but we needed to be able to speak into their core concepts with an expertise of understanding. We needed to understand their language and be geared to the movement of expression that each brings into the counseling experience. In the counseling world, we would need to talk the talk of these theories.

Our course of study at the time was focused more on the biblical ideas of counseling. We were required to learn how to counsel people with classes such as counseling from the Psalms, counseling from the gospels, counseling with the words of Jesus, counseling from the writings of Paul, and many more. We were taught how to listen to individuals tell their story. Sometimes, compelled by pain, grief, or calm reassurance, these individuals would share their lives with us. We would then practice ways of directing the person into some biblical thought process with words like, "You need to learn how to act like a new person who is deeply loved by God" (this can be very close to behavioral or attachment theory). Or we might suggest, "You need to renew your thinking through the power of the Holy Spirit" (this can be a very close relative to the cognitive theory). But our focus was always on the biblical practices and concepts; not the current

Psychology of the day, even though we had studied the theories, and understood the concepts and languages of each one.

Unfortunately, spiritual transformation was not a class, or even a directed study. Transformation might have been an underlining theme but only because it was a sound biblical truth, not because it was a purposeful, planned study. That one day in Dr. Bertram's class changed the focus for me. I began to think about helping people with their transformational journey. I began to speak about this concept with others. Through that process, I learned some interesting and very helpful things.

One of the first things I learned was that most people do not understand what genuine spiritual transformation is. They have never been taught the idea, concept, or total scope of this personal journey. In fact, I wasn't sure I understood it.

Like a lot of people, I was more used to the term *sanctification*. I understood this as the process of growing into a holy person, because God is holy, and we should become more like Him. I was taught that we never fully accomplish this process until we reach heaven. We are to continue to grow toward that end, but we will not achieve total success until we enter eternity. But the only day-to-day instructions I remembered were: read and study your Bible, pray, and stay faithful to your local church. As far as I could understand at the time, I was true to those instructions, and I knew many others who worshiped with me on a regular basis were also following those guidelines. But in spite of those good instructions, and our personal effort, the struggles of agreeing in like-mindedness within the congregation were always painfully obvious.

The transformation I'm talking about is not about the terms of today—for example, being transformed through a day at the beauty shop, producing a new hairstyle, new nails, or a look that totally changes your appearance. This is not about hiring a personal trainer who will teach you how to lose fifty pounds through hard work, exercise, and healthy eating. It's not finding the right clothing sale, or personal tailor, allowing you to purchase a new closet full of outfits that make your friends marvel and comment about how different you look. Although each of these may be great in what they do for your personal health and well-being, they are not the deeper, genuine spiritual transformation that we are talking about and that I have felt the need to explore for so much of my adult life.

To help me with this deeper understanding, I began to focus on the biblical approach, using Romans 12:2 as my main source:

> Do not conform any longer to the pattern of this world,
> but be transformed by the renewing of your mind ...
> (NIV)

The terminology of this verse, and others like it, seemed to speak differently than what I was trying to do at the time. It seemed like a real relationship could exist between walking the path of life, and at the same time, becoming a new person who is like Christ. It also clearly defines a way of achieving the goal by "renewing" my mind. This concept also seemed to fit with my previous study of psychological theories and biblical application, but I had to go deeper. I began to read many commentaries on this verse. Dr. Jack Cottrell's *Commentary on Romans* helped me the most. Cottrell says:

> Paul emphatically commands us **not** to shape our lives according to the anti-Christian cultures of this world, but to continue allowing ourselves to be recreated according to God's will, a process which began in the act of regeneration (Rom.6:1-11) and which continues through the truth of his Word and the power of his Spirit ... which means that the change in view is not

> something we do or can do for ourselves; it is something that is done to us. Thus the transformation (and the renewing) can be accomplished by God alone ... We have the responsibility of desiring the change and consenting to it and yielding ourselves up to the power of the Holy Spirit within us.[1]

Yes! These words made sense to me. I now understood that I have a direct responsibility and God has a responsibility. I must *want* this, but God is the one in charge. Together we use the truth of His word, and the power of His Spirit, to shape our lives away from this world's pull and toward transformation. This is biblical direction that applies cognitive theory, behavior theory, and, most importantly, the power of God's Spirit. This was in no way about losing fifty pounds, or purchasing a new suit of clothes. This is change from the inside out.

My next step was to learn how to use this new understanding. It seemed like the day-to-day process could be the same as I had been taught in the past. Reading and studying the Bible helped me know more about Christ and His ways. Prayer helped me feel good about communicating with God, but I felt little growth. Even with the little growth I had, how was I to measure it? Some days felt good; I believed I was on the right path. Some days were not so good; I felt discouraged or even defeated. True transformation began to seem like words read from a page, and obtaining whatever that should look like in real life was just a dream. Besides, I had ministry to do. I was serving as a full-time pastor and part-time counselor. I was busy and couldn't allow myself to get bogged down in personal criticism based on some form of an unattainable goal.

However, during this time of struggle when I learned how to

---

[1] Jack Cottrell, *The College Press NIV Commentary: Romans Vol. 2* (Joplin: College Press, 1998), 314.

use this new understanding personally, I was beginning to share the concept of transformation with other counselors within the counseling field. I saw that the idea of genuine transformation could work in a very positive manner within a counseling setting. Their feedback gave me hope. I believed that we needed to further the idea while learning how to develop its scope and overall procedure, even though this concept seemed quite new and different than what we had been taught.

CHAPTER 3
Finding the Right Map

At the end of the day, direction, not intention,
determines destination.
—Andy Stanley, *The Principle of the Path*

In 1990, my wife, Dewenia, and I and our son, Josh, took a wonderful vacation. We left our home in Indiana and drove to the Badlands of South Dakota. We spent a day at Mt. Rushmore, then drove through the flatlands of Wyoming and south to Estes Park, just north of Denver, Colorado. We stayed in a magnificent cabin built right on the edge of the Fall River Gorge. The highlight of our trip was a horseback ride to Odessa Lake, one of the highest elevated lakes in the continental United States. The entire trip was a marvelous adventure. And it was possible because, before we left home, we bought a Rand McNally map, hardcover edition.

We needed a good map. We didn't have Google, or phone apps, and we didn't know anything about having screens on a car's dashboard that would tell us when to make every turn. These new mapping skills might have been available for some, but at the time, we had never heard of them. We used what we had. We planned each day's travel using the best technique we knew. In those days, a lot of our travel was done by the seat of our pants. We studied our map, we stopped more than once to ask directions, and we seldom called ahead for a motel. We did fine for the most part. There was, however, a time in Wyoming where we nearly ran out of gasoline. We learned, through the miles, that Wyoming is a big place with a lot of fuel-guzzling miles between towns. We could see that on the map, but we didn't truly understand it until we lived it. We were also somewhat anxious as we traversed Colorado and had to drive the winding roads around the Rocky Mountains after dark, in the rain. We were looking for our cabin, which was the only reservation we'd made ahead of time. We were redeemed when we finally found that cabin through the curves, twists, and uncertainty of the all-day drive to get there. We were happy to jump out of our car and run through the rain and inside to the safety and shelter of the pine walls and tin roof. We could not, however, imagine the beauty of the picturesque view until the next morning when the sun magnified the towering trees, the rapids of the river, and the total glory of the mountain scenery. Our map had served its purpose.

With this idea in mind, I believed that we needed some sort of map to revolutionize the transformation experience of people, both in the counseling office and in day-to-day life. We needed something new—something up-to-date and original. I was searching for something like a map to guide me in my duties as a resident counselor. I was having discussions with the directors of our counseling program at Crucible Counseling, and they explained to me that the style of counseling being used by most of their counselors was different than mine. These other knowledgeable and effective counselors knew the theories of psychology well, and they practiced them during their counseling sessions; however, from their perspective, my focus seemed to be more on the biblical concepts, with the transformation of the client being my number one goal. My superiors asked if I could work with the other counselors and teach them this style, opening an entirely new door for me. I was glad to walk through it even though I was somewhat apprehensive. I was, after all, still struggling with understanding my own transformation journey. My personal question was: How could I produce, and share, legitimate and helpful information with others?

To achieve this goal, and map a new plan, we started with the basics and developed what we called the "L-Quad System":

Look

Listen

Learn

Leave

Look

Before you enter the counseling office, with any client, *look* at yourself. How is your personal faith today? Are you comfortable with your knowledge and ability to teach the basic doctrines of God, grace, and forgiveness? Before you attempt to help others, make sure you are right with God, and with Jesus as your Savior.

Listen

Listen for the faith-based statements of your clients; they will tell you the place in which they stand with their own faith.

Learn

Learn to take this faith-based statement and help your client by sharing some scripture, Bible concept, or relevant biblical story that will help them get one step closer to God.

Leave

Pray for, or with, your client. This may or may not be done at the end of your session, but it needs to be done by you, for your client, at some time. Make it your practice to demand that the Holy Spirit be in charge of each and every session.

(More information about the "L-Quad" can be found at www. targetingtransformation.com.)

When we activated this system, it became our new mapping plan. It also took on a whole new life of its own. As I began to meet with the other counselors on a one-to-one basis, I learned more about how to teach this process. These students of theory challenged me, and each other, in many ways. Some of them had their own strong base of faith to work from; others were marginal at best in their spiritual development. So in many ways, we learned together. We began to develop language that helped us understand how to hear people's faith-based statements, and then to relate those statements to where they were on the journey of transformation. We realized that, to take each person to a new level of understanding in their personal journey, we had to incorporate our existing biblical concepts in creative ways. We knew that some people would immediately accept direct biblical truth, while others needed more time, and gentle wording, in order to accept the same biblical concepts into their lives.

We were laboring to help others in their Christian walk. We were obligated to learn how to administer this instructional language in the most productive manner. We needed to remember that each person we encountered would receive this information differently. We had to take the time to get to know each person, and his or her unique circumstances, and then develop a trusting interaction with him or her. This is another reason why we needed to plead for the Holy Spirit to be the leader in our sessions.

We also learned that we had no real measure of understanding about where each person was on the spiritual journey of transformation. We had no qualifying measure for how to rate each encounter, but we had to move forward the best we could. Then we found a great help. We discovered a book entitled *Maximum*

Faith: Live Like Jesus by George Barna. Barna's thoughts gave us the clarity and direction we'd been unable to find anywhere else.

Transformation Map

In Barna's book, he outlines what he defines as a road map of the journey of faith, or what he titles the Ten Stops. This concept was developed after six years of surveys from some fifteen thousand people across North America. Through these surveys, and the study of their results, Barna developed a qualifying place, with a name, for each stop on the journey. Barna also gave us a more practical way of understanding spiritual transformation.

Barna explains the process this way;

> True spiritual transformation is impossible unless you become fully dependent upon God. Fully dependent. No human being is capable of producing spiritual transformation in their own life. God must pilot and control the process. Your job is to want this so badly that you become determined to cooperate fully with Him.[2]

Barna is not defining the word *transformation* as I have from the Romans 12:2 text. Instead, he challenges us to place the definition into action and uses the language of everyday life to do so. This understanding helped me turn a corner, and to see an entirely new road ahead. Now I could bring this concept into the counseling office, and hopefully, expand it further into everyday life.

But I was also able to double-up on the concepts I received from the Romans text. We must *want* this transformation in our lives. We must want it to the point of becoming determined to

---

[2] George Barna, *Maximum Faith: Live Like Jesus* (Austin: Fedd and Company, 2011), 14.

follow through with it. We must want it to the point of being willing to let God have control while allowing ourselves to become totally dependent on Him. This is a solid biblical concept that offered me much more clarity and direction, as well as the ability to more clearly express the idea to others.

Barna's map is explained in the Ten Stops:

1. **Ignorant of sin:** Not understanding or knowing anything about sin.
2. **Aware:** We become aware of sin, but do nothing about it, or its effect on our lives.
3. **Concerned:** We become concerned about the sin in our lives and seek some answers for our concern.
4. **Forgiveness:** The concern leads us to find a person who can forgive our sins, and we accept Jesus Christ as the only one who can do so.
5. **Active:** The acceptance of Jesus as Savior leads us to fellowship, worship, and serve in a local faith-based community of like-minded believers.
6. **Holy Discontent:** We become discontent with merely attending church and believe that God has more for us.
7. **Brokenness:** We enter into a partnership with God that permits God to break us of sin, self, and society.
8. **Surrender:** We allow God to have complete control of our lives.
9. **Love of God:** We learn to love God completely and understand how much Jesus did for us on the cross.
10. **Love of People:** We learn how to see people through God's eyes and love each person completely.

These Ten Stops gave us an outline to work with that we'd never had before. It gave us some direction of thought that we could then discuss. If a person's faith-based statement was, "I am really discontent with the church right now," we might want to proceed with a challenge to the person of moving forward in the journey. As always, this would depend on the individual and which way he or she was headed in his or her progression of transformation. But now we had something to gauge the process. We could begin to speak to the possibility that this person might be at Stop 6, Holy Discontent. If that was the case, then we could now have conversation about moving forward into Brokenness, or Stop 7. That was a revolutionary talk for us.

Barna's stops were not, and are not, a concrete measure that works every time. But it was, and is, a great guide—far above anything else we'd seen. We could begin the discussion in our own minds and then present the possibilities to the client. Together, then, we could unlock more insight into whether the client was moving closer to God or was slipping away from God because of a personal issue. This knowledge began to help a lot of our clients. It became a reliable map, a guide in understanding transformation, and a way to ask the right questions along the journey.

The other thing we could do was to judge where we were as counselors. We could ask ourselves: How does my life fit within these stops? Am I comfortable at Stop 5, being active in the local church and serving others, but not really attempting to move up into a total Love of God (Stop 9) or Fully Loving People (Stop 10)? These questions about my own journey began to challenge me as church pastor, and not just as a counselor. What direction have I given to others in the past, and will I continue to give them the same instructions in the future?

To help me get some direction on this dilemma, I began to share the Barna information with other ministers, and through that process, we were blessed with a graph that looked something like this.

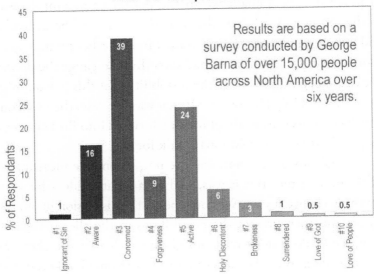

Ten Stops Graph

For us, this graph allowed us to see that most people on the spiritual journey of transformation never get more than halfway to the goal of achieving the top spots. We all start at Ignorant of Sin (Stop 1). Then, by the grace of God we find Jesus, (Stop 4), and eventually get settled in at Stop 5, Active in Church. The numbers also show that from Stop 1 through Stop 5 we see about 89 percent of the people who answered Barna's survey; 89 percent stay within the first five stops while only 11 percent reach the higher levels. Why is it so difficult to move on to Stop 6 and beyond? Maybe I, and others like me, have hindered people in this process? Not because we are malicious or evil, but because we just didn't have a more direct understanding and measure of spiritual success. We didn't have, or know how to use, the most current map.

For instance, if a person came into my office while I was

serving as the minister of a local church and suggested that they were "uncomfortable" with their lives in the church, I might ask them what "uncomfortable" means to them.

They might answer, "It's just not enough. God seems to want more from me."

With that understanding, in the past, I would talk with them about getting involved in a deeper Bible study, a short-term mission trip, or leading a ministry team that I knew needed encouragement and direction. I might ask about their current Bible reading, prayer time, and personal devotions. All these personal disciplines are important, and shouldn't be overlooked; however, these disciplines, or the lack thereof, may not be the core issue for every individual, and therefore, may not help the believer move forward in his or her transformation journey. I may have been helping them remain stuck at Stop 5. At the time, I was not a good person to ask for directions because I didn't have knowledge of a better map. I was simply giving the best information I had.

Today, I might suggest something deeper to an individual who is "uncomfortable." I'm more likely to share with them the previous chart. Then, with suggestions like; "Is it possible that God Himself is giving you this feeling of discontentment? If so, can you see yourself moving forward on your journey of transformation?" Now we have language that is different from the past. Now we can see a qualified measure of spiritual success for the individual and not just limit him or her to local church activities. This may be troublesome to a lot of church people, but we need to be realistic with the lives of people who come to us with questions. We may have the responsibility of directing these people on their transformation journey, but we cannot hold them back because of our personal ideas of success. We need to stay focused on the other person's spiritual journey, his or her target of transformation, and his or her personal success in reaching genuine transformation.

As Barna discusses in his work, the church mostly measures success by three things: (1) attendance, (2) budgets, and (3) buildings. We see our churches as successful if they have a good or growing attendance, strong budgets (which they are reaching), and larger buildings. But is that what Christ died for? No.

When Jesus died and was raised from the dead, He gave birth to the church. The church started boldly and directly on the Day of Pentecost (three thousand souls baptized that day). In the book of Revelation, the church is defined as "The Bride of Christ" (Revelation 19:7 NLT). In no way should we weaken the need for and strong direction of the church in history, or its current need within our life, or our society as a whole. We should all do our part to help the church grow stronger. However, it is possible for us to assign too much authority to the church and take away from the spiritual journey of individual believers. Jesus's words to people who asked Him which commandments are the greatest were these:

> You must love The Lord your God with all your heart, all your soul, and all you mind. This is the first and greatest commandment. A second is equally important: Love your neighbor as yourself. (Matthew 22:37–39 NLT)

When I place this commandment of Jesus alongside the Ten Stops of Faith, I can see that they have agreement on where we as believers need to go; however, I do not see the proper correlation with the current success goals inside most of today's churches. Reaching the highest pinnacle of this commandment should be our transformation goal. Why wouldn't the church want to help all people become the living proof of this great commandment? I believe if the church leadership does this for individuals, we will also see a great awakening of truly spiritual leaders within our congregations. Churches will then see spiritual growth in measurable, magnificent ways. This process can then become a transformation revolution because we are now able to use a new, more accurate map as a guide toward the target.

CHAPTER 4
Transformation DIET Plan

What God asks us to do, He equips us to do.
—Dutch Sheets, *Watchman Prayer*

To start a transformation journey, you will need a map and then a plan. This plan needs be led by the power of God's word, and then implemented into your life. You can follow the idea from the text of Romans 12:2, which again clearly states that transformation starts with the "renewing" of your mind, and *not* following the ways of this world.

To renew our minds, we should consider a passage from Romans 8:10 that states, "Since Christ lives within you, even though your body will die because of sin, your spirit is alive because you have been made right with God." I believe verses like this one can help you use a different frame of mind to get a clearer picture of the right things to consume for life. For instance, during my continual journey of understanding transformation I realized one great challenge: life can be busy. Sometimes it is genuinely busy, with many things competing for your attention, and at other times, you make life busy just because. So, how do I help myself, and others throughout life, to stay in ministry positions and to prosper in this busy stream of life and duty? I came up with the following formula for success, which, if followed, will enhance the opportunity of targeting transformation.

$$(DIET + QT) \times HS = r1021m$$

Here's what this formula means: know the *DIET of brokenness and find a place where you can hear God whisper (QT). When we multiply these things by being totally consumed by the Holy Spirit (HS) we get Romans 10:21 ministry.*

This idea is based on the text of Romans 10:21, in which Paul spoke from the mind of God:

> All day long I have held out my hands to a disobedient
> and obstinate people. (NIV)

Paul, throughout this chapter of Romans, and the previous ones, shares and molds his heart with God's heart. The genuine mercy of God becomes clear because God has shown the love He has for the people of Israel by using the illustration of a man holding out his hands all day long. This is tiring, and it will wear you out. God, however, has never dropped His arms. He has never quit, even though the people He loves continue to be obstinate and disobedient. This same concept is used in the writing of the prophet Isaiah. Isaiah 65:2 says:

> All day long I have held out my hands to an obstinate
> people, who walk in ways not good, pursuing their own
> imaginations. (NIV)

Generation after generation, God stays faithful to a people who are disobedient and pursue their own ways more than God's. From the Old Testament prophet to the New Testament writer, the concept remains.

So I wonder: what if we do the same? How long can you hold out your hands as far as you can reach? Try this. Can you hold out your hands - all the way out - for one minute? Ten minutes? One hour? It's tiring, isn't it? In fact, I question if you were even willing to do it for thirty seconds. What if we take this verse and apply these life skills to our ministries? All day long—for as long as we do ministry—we hold out our hands to the people we serve. This also is tiring and requires great mercy and strength. Yet we have God Himself as our example, and we are striving to be like Him. To be successful in ministry, and in life, we must pursue this journey to reach genuine spiritual transformation.

It is my purest belief that, to survive and grow in ministry today, in the way this text illustrates, whether full-time staff or church volunteer, each person needs to *know* one thing, and *do* two things.

The Diet of Brokenness (DIET)

We all need to know and understand brokenness because we live in a broken world. To help understand this concept I like to use the acronym of DIET. Nobody likes the term *diet*, but this is not about food and our bodies. This is a concept about paying attention to what enters our minds—to what we consume as followers of Christ. When we use this concept, we can map out a plan to understand four areas that, for every Christian, lead from death to life.

D. *Disobedience causes brokenness.*

In the book of Genesis, we are told that God created a beautiful place for humankind and desired a close relationship with them. God went from His Spirit hovering about the darkness into creating the sun, moon, stars, vegetation, land, sea, animals, and man. This was a magnificent and miraculous manifestation of

God as Creator, and for God as a living being who wanted a relationship with humankind.

However, God gave humankind a couple of simple rules, which Adam and Eve, as we came to know them, quickly broke. Because of humankind's disobedience, God sent them out of His garden. God's punishment was to separate humankind from Himself. This created a division between God and humankind. We call this division sin. The close relationship God wanted has been broken because God cannot be around sin. God has a plan to bring the relationship back together, but the world we live in today is broken. (You may want to see Romans 8 for some insight on life and death and restoring your personal relationship.)

Because of this sin between God and humankind, we now are born into a broken world. Every child is born into this broken state. Each child inherits the sin of his parents, starting with Adam and Eve. This new child has committed no sin, but it is merely what he or she is born into. This broken relationship affects each of us. You cannot minimize the effects of sin in your life. This brokenness of disobedience is real, and it keeps us from God.

I. *Internal Brokenness*

There is also an internal brokenness within each human being. This may be the most silent, most elusive part of brokenness. We are so engaged with personal pride, ego, and humanistic belief systems that we have a difficult time realizing that God hates pride. Proverbs 8:13 states clearly that God hates pride. Pride keeps us away from God's ways and God's plan. Pride creates an even greater void between humankind and God because humankind begins to think more of himself than of God. Humanistic thought teaches that man is the center of all things and that humankind has the ability to take care of all of our own issues and problems. This is a direct insult to Christianity, which teaches that God is the creator and sustainer of humankind, and only He should be the center of worship because only He has the answers. This internal struggle is etched deep into the brain of humankind and should be understood as an area of brokenness that each and every person needs to address.

E. *External Brokenness.*

Life also provides many outside sources that can break us—for example, when a person loses his or her job and it is months before the income can be replaced, causing debt in the process. Or a time in which we are invested heavily in the stock market for our retirement plans or personal money management funds that go bust. It hurts, and through what may be no fault of our own, our lives can be broken for years.

There's also a brokenness that centers around relationships. When we love and care for another person and he or she deceives us, lies to us, or cheats on us, we can suffer a broken spirit that may last for years and may take a great deal of love, prayer, and understanding to reach any kind of healing in our lives. In some cases, healing never happens, and we remain in this broken state for the rest of our lives.

The brokenness of health or death can, in many ways, be the most devastating for us to live with and manage in our lives. When a person who has loved us for our entire lives is taken from us, it hurts. The suddenness can break us in the most devastating way. Then there's brokenness that side-slaps us like cancer, or some other destructive and devastating health issues that seem to come from nowhere. Once again, this slides into our lives from external dimensions. They may or may not happen because of some bad decision that we make, or because of life in general. Regardless, they can break us.

In 1974, I lost my father after he had a heart attack. I was broken and angry. I was angry because my father was a very loving and caring individual who did not need to leave this earth at forty-seven years old. I was angry because I wanted very much to have him involved in the farming business, which I had taken over just one year before. I was angry because my wife was pregnant with our second son, and my dad never got to meet him. I was angry because God let this happen. The only way I knew how to fight through my broken spirit was to work, so I poured myself into it. I figured that, if I kept busy, I wouldn't have to think so much about my anger. It took at least two years before I finally let that anger go. It took so much time to realize that my father did not want to die, and that God was not somehow mad at me, or punishing my family for some grave sin. My brokenness in life was real.

Then, in 2001, my wife and I lost our eldest son, Joseph, to cancer. He was only twenty-nine. I was not angry; I was sad—the kind of sad that develops as you begin to see a dark cloud forming overhead and slowly, skillfully, and determinately bringing itself down around you until it encompasses your entire being, preventing you from moving or thinking. I was sad because I could not escape that darkness, because Joe had a nine-year-old son who needed a father, and because I believed that, if my son could beat the cancer, he could become a powerful spokesman to give God praise. Instead of a reasonable future for my family and myself, I felt only deep brokenness, but during this loss, unlike that of my father's death, my faith was stronger. My relationship with Christ had grown through the years, and even through the darkest times, I knew the Lord's light was there somewhere. Brokenness was present, but so was hope.

Life has a way of dealing to all of us these kinds of brokenness. Anyone reading these words, who has lived a few years of life, has known one or more of these. You can blame God, or another person, or yourself. Or you can concede that God may be teaching you something through these difficult experiences. Either way, you can most certainly be broken by the external forces of life.

So far, we have three letters in DIET, spelling DIE. It is important that we acknowledge that each of these areas of brokenness leads to death; therefore, we need the fourth letter, adding a positive outcome to DIE.

T. *Transformation Brokenness.*
The transformation brokenness is the key to targeting transformation in both your own personal journey to be like Christ, and the idea of you speaking into the transformation of each person you meet, each day of your life.

This brokenness has two main points. The first is partnership. This is a partnership between you and God. You agree to partner with God for your good and your growth. God is waiting for this agreement, and He wants it very much. The second is that there is a choice. God has made His choice; He sent Jesus. Jesus made His choice; He died so that you could have life. Now it is your choice to focus on your transformation and on consuming the right things for your growth and your long-term health.

When you make this choice, you choose to partner with Christ in order to break you in three areas of your life: sin, self, and society. Each of these three relate to the brokenness listed above.

(1) *Sin* is the brokenness of this world created by *disobedience.* Transformation is a choice to stop the sin in your life. Without God's partnership, this is not possible. You will need the Spirit of Christ to give you the power to conquer sin.

(2) *Self* is the *internal* battle of pride and ego. You will show this to God and ask for Him to extend His grace to break

this self-centeredness. Transformation is a process that requires each person to break his or her own pride and seek only to honor our God.

(3) *Society* gives many *external* thought processes that need to be broken. Transformation is the key that will allow you to think about your thinking. Think about what has entered into your mind and what continues to be permitted.

This DIET Plan is the one essential thing to know. Now, let's look at the two things you must *do*.

Targeting Quiet Time (QT)

The first thing to do is: *Find a place where you can hear God whisper.*

This idea is based on the life of the prophet Elijah, which we find in 1 Kings 17–19. Elijah is a true man of God who spoke the words of God to the earthly leaders of his day. God cared for Elijah, and Elijah followed the direction of God. Elijah went from a mountaintop experience on Mount Carmel (1 Kings 18:1–40) into a time of low depression (1 Kings 19:1–18). During this time of depression, God led him to Mt. Horeb and asked him a very important question: "What are you doing here, Elijah?"

Elijah replied that he had zealously served the Lord, but the people he was sent to serve were disobedient, broke God's commands, and had killed all the other prophets. He was alone, and the people were trying to kill him (1 Kings 19:10).

Elijah speaks from the past directly into the heart of many men and women who faithfully serve God today. They work hard, because there is much to do. They can and do have fabulous mountaintop experiences that are amazing; however, they are too often rewarded for their labors by words that bring harm, pain, or fear. It is not uncommon to feel the need to run and get away, and it is very common, as Elijah did, to feel all alone.

But God did an amazing thing for Elijah. God sent a mighty wind that shook the rocks on the mountain where Elijah was, but God was not in the wind. God then developed an earthquake that shook the ground where Elijah stood, but God was not in the earthquake. Then God sent a fierce fire across the mountain, but God was not in the fire (1 Kings 19:11–12). Then, and only then, God gently whispered: "What are you doing here, Elijah?"

It is that whisper that we need to hear. We who serve others in ministry positions need to find this place of quiet daily. When we do, like Elijah, God will share His heart with us. God is not going to compete with the noise of today, or the self-imposed business of our times. But He longs to lift up His arms and place them around us in the quiet time of prayer and communication with Him. Being quiet before God will reap large rewards. Like Elijah, God will speak into our needs and our ministry direction. God said to Elijah: I have a job for you (go anoint some kings), I will get you some help (Elisha), and you are not alone (there are at least seven hundred others who serve Yahweh). Why would He not do the same for us today? Why wouldn't these times of gently speaking be most likely to happen during a quiet time where we are waiting to hear Him whisper? To serve well in ministry, we need a quiet time to hear God whisper.

Targeting Holy Spirit (HS)

The second thing to do is: *Become totally consumed by the Holy Spirit.*

In the fourteenth chapter of John, Jesus is preparing the disciples for His death. He labors to share the idea that He is going, and they will not see Him again, but He will send a new counselor, the Holy Spirit, to them after He is gone. The Holy

Spirit will replace Him, and the Spirit will be in them, never to leave. The Spirit will then guide them into all truth.

The disciples resisted this change. They knew Jesus, and they wanted Jesus to stay. He was flesh and bone that they knew and accepted. He'd shown great compassion and strength, and in their minds, He shouldn't have had to go. But He must because better was coming, and the disciples needed to accept the change and ready themselves for it.

We, as today's believers and disciples, often do, think, and say the same things the disciples of Jesus's day said, thought, and did. When we accept Jesus as our Savior and Lord, His Holy Spirit is given as a gift (Acts 2:38). This Spirit now dwells in us. But how much authority do we give Him? He will consume us if we allow; however, we, like previous disciples, become comfortable with ourselves. The flesh and bone we have become normal for us. We want to keep what we have. We reason that the person we are, in spite of our shortcomings, whom we have known our entire lives, is doing all right. Why should we have to allow the Spirit to have complete control? Yet, that is what is asked of us.

I have known many individuals in the ministry who talk about God's Spirit leading them; however, there appears to be little outward evidence in their lives. "The heart is deceitful above all things and beyond cure. Who can understand it?" (Jeremiah 17:9, NIV). This is a true and clear verse. We as humans hold ourselves in high esteem. Ministry can, and does, promote the personal image of grandeur. Speaking to groups and hearing their accolades becomes addictive to the flesh. But the apostle Paul constantly reminds us to beware of those cravings (Galatians 5:16–21), while kindly giving us a list of the fruit we should see if we are totally living in the Spirit (Galatians 5:22–23). Paul also relates well the idea of being totally consumed by the Spirit. He uses these words:

> If we are living now by the Holy Spirit, let us follow the
> Holy Spirit's leading in every part of our lives. (Galatians
> 5:25 NLT)

"Every part" is no less than totally consumed. The verse is focused on living in such a manner that we allow the Spirit to lead us completely. Then, when we do, His Spirit will be seen as the one who is leading us in each and every part of our lives. We need this inspired leading if we are serious about continuing in ministry positions within our churches today.

Jim Cymbala, the highly successful pastor of Brooklyn Tabernacle, speaks into this very idea in his book *Fresh Wind, Fresh Fire* with a chapter entitled "Too Smart for Our Own Good?" Here is how Cymbala starts the chapter:

> Often when our Pastoral staff meets together, amid the flurry of busy days and what the world would term 'church success'—a large membership, nearly twenty branch churches, the choir performing at Billy Graham crusades, our videos being televised nationwide, invitations to speak here and there—a nagging thought from The Lord spreads across the edges of our hearts: *Remember who has done all this. Your need for me hasn't lessened at all.* [3]

Jim Cymbala totally gets it, and so should we. We need to be able to step away from ourselves and be consumed by the Holy Spirit. He will then be allowed to make things happen.

So, you have the formula. One thing you must know: *DIET,* and two things you must do: *Find a place where you can hear God whisper (QT), and be totally consumed by the Holy Spirit (HS).* All of this works in a day-to-day life plan based on the formula: (DIET + QT) x HS = r1021m.

---

[3] Jim Cymbala, *Fresh Wind, Fresh Fire* (Grand Rapids: Zondervan, 1997), 157.

CHAPTER 5
Hearing the Statements

Every time we say yes to God we will get a little more
sensitive to hearing him the next time.
—John Ortberg, *God is Closer Than You Think*

Now that we have knowledge of DIET, and the "r1021m formula," we can put these concepts to work in many ways in our day-to-day lives. This information isn't just for full-time ministers, although I believe it will help them greatly as they serve and lead their individual congregations, but it also works for any person who is trying to live the Christian life and move toward God in their own transformation journey. Let me give you some examples of what I call "faith-based" statements. These "faith-based" statements are words we hear from other people, which give us a strong clue as to where that person is on their journey of faith.

Sharon's Faith-Based Statement

I met a lady I will call Sharon (not her actual name) in the counseling office. She was sent to me with a diagnosis of depression. Sharon certainly had the symptoms of depression, and from her vantage point, life was hopeless. She was barely able to keep her job, she had suffered through a nasty divorce, which was not by her choice, and most of her current relationships were struggling.

But through her story, she gave me one faith-based statement that I believed we could work with.

"I think God is mad at me."

From that statement, I had some direction to move forward with. It was my thought that Sharon was in Stop 5 on the Barna map. She was active in church. However, she was not moving forward into any feelings of discontent (Stop 6). She was stagnant at best, or even in danger of moving backward on her transformation journey. Not forgetting, of course, that my goal was to help her in her personal journey of transformation, this statement gave me a basis of action to develop a plan for her. From listening to her sad story, I didn't blame her for being depressed. The main question I had for her was, "How long do you want to stay depressed?" I needed her to accept the fact that there was a way out of her depression. I also needed her to accept the idea that getting out of this hopelessness wouldn't be easy, but it was attainable. Once we were together on those two concepts, we could move forward.

Sharon needed a counselor—not just me, a flesh and bone person speaking into her life, but also the true Counselor, God's Spirit, who was at this time unseen by Sharon, but who was going to be the real light in her life long after she and I stopped meeting. My job was to take her faith-based statement and show her the fallacy of those words. Even though she felt as though God was mad at her, there was no biblical truth to support that feeling.

I walked slowly with Sharon until she was strong enough to realize that, in spite of the drama that was controlling her mind, she was still a dear child of God whom He still loved completely. Once she accepted her true relationship with God (which she had been willing to do at other times in her life), her relationships, her job, and her mind started on the path of being healthy again.

This change came about as the result of a faith-based statement, and someone willing to help Sharon grow closer to God. It took time, but it was well worth the effort, and there was never a guarantee that Sharon's depression wouldn't return. But after much effort on Sharon's part, she learned to speak with different words about God and her relationship with Him. That movement represents a key part of her transformation journey.

Jesus Hears from the Crowd

One of the greatest examples of a person hearing the faith-based statement of others and using it for that person's benefit, and God's glory, is Jesus. He was the Master in so many ways. In the New Living Translation of John 6:28, the faith-based statement made to Jesus is: *"What does God want us to do?"*

Here is a case where Jesus is followed by great crowds, and He says to the people, "You are following me because I fed you (yesterday), not because you saw some miraculous signs. But now (today), I would like to give you the Bread of Life (Me)." The crowd then wanted to debate about how Moses fed the Israelite nation during their forty years in the desert; therefore, they (the current descendants) deserve to be fed now. Jesus clarifies their scriptural understanding with the idea that it was God, not Moses, who fed them mana through those years. He continues with the idea that what God wants now is for them to accept Him, the Bread of Life, which is eternal life, not just a temporary meal. Jesus gives them a biblical clarification, preceded by a faith-based statement. This statement initiated the rest of the conversation. Jesus was great at this. How did this interaction affect the transformation of those who were listening to Jesus? I believe it brought them one step closer to understanding (or being like) Him. Because individuals in the crowd knew and understood more about Jesus and what He was doing, they could get closer to Him, and become more like Him.

If you continue to read about this interaction, you will see that many that day stopped following Jesus. Many left Him because His wording confused them. Jesus began to talk about eating His body and drinking His blood. He wanted them to have a deeper and more spiritual mind-set than they were willing to obtain at the time. His real motivation was to get people to trust Him. How could they understand eternal life, given by the Bread of Life, if they could not get past thinking about a free meal today? However, those who stayed grew in their likeness to Him. Their faith grew, so Jesus was successful in speaking into the faith-based statement.

One thing we must remember. This encounter with Jesus—or the ones we will have—represent a one-time encounter. The people who walk away may have more encounters in the future; who knows what God's Spirit might do for them? Perhaps there is another person who will speak to them whose goal is to help them on their journey of transformation. How do we know? Success comes in doing our part—each person, each encounter, each and every day.

Faith-Based Statement from Chris

I met Chris in the counseling office; he was struggling with his marriage. Chris and his wife were seeing another counselor together each week and had been for some time; however, forward progress was stagnant. The other counselor had called me and asked me to meet with Chris by himself. She felt that Chris needed another man to speak into his life, and she was frustrated that most of the time in the couple's therapy was spent with the couple arguing and name-calling.

Chris didn't need a counselor, but instead, simply another male who could hear his pain, and share his frustration. He was bitter and hurt, and during many sessions, he just needed to unload that pain. Chris had a faith in God that was being shared in his local church, and the couple was still attending worship services together. However, outside of the church building, they mostly fought or simply avoided each other. I found it difficult to get a clear picture of where he was in his spiritual walk because there were many confusing statements. Then he a made statement that gave me pause: *"I think it's time to give up on my marriage and find a real Christian woman."*

This was a clear statement of faith but based on some very poor theology. I assured Chris that if he divorced his wife, I would not think less of him. I would still be his friend, and I would do my best to help him be strong during the divorce. However, I did encourage him to think about other options. It seemed to me that Chris was struggling with his own personal spiritual journey and could not see any forward direction because of the anger in his present marital dilemma. Divorce was not going to solve his issues, or bring him closer to God, which was still my number one goal. In fact, I believed that any legal action against his wife would send him backward in his transformation journey.

I began to ask Chris if he thought God had placed him in this marriage because He wanted Chris's life to be easy, or maybe God had placed him in this marriage so Chris could learn patience and how to love another person in a way that he could not learn in any other way. We struggled with that concept for many weeks as Chris began to evaluate his own life. He needed to battle through a long, winding road with this particular part of his struggle.

In the process, Chris grew as a man, and as a believer, and I saw how God began to work in his life. Chris allowed God's Spirit to bring him a calmness that only comes through Christ, and a peace that only comes through true grace. We began to pray together for God's direction as a husband, and specifically for Chris's wife. Then one day Chris came in to my office with a look of total joy, and he said these words, "God has changed my wife!" We stopped right there and gave God praise! Chris went on to explain how his wife had changed into a more loving person and that the two of them were communicating, holding each other, and planning for the future in ways that had been lost between them for so long. It was an astonishing change, and an answer to our prayer. Because one statement of faith was heard, evaluated, and developed in another person's life, an entire family received the benefit.

Jesus Hears the Rich Young Ruler

Another example of this from the life of Jesus is in Mark 10, when Jesus has an encounter with a wealthy man. This man walked up to Jesus, speaking words from his heart: *Good teacher, what should I do to get eternal life?"*

This faith-based statement came in the form of a question. The young man essentially said, "I know I need, and I want, eternal life, so how do I achieve it?" Jesus speaks directly to the question by suggesting a biblical understanding about keeping the commandments, to which the young man says that he has followed these commandments since he was a boy. Then, and only then, Jesus challenges this man with a slightly stronger message. Jesus tells the young man to get rid of anything that would stop him from following Jesus. In this man's case, this means all of his possessions. The text tells us that, upon hearing this directive from Jesus, the man sadly walked away. The man, in effect, said no, but I completely believe that the intent of Jesus was to get this man closer to God. Did He fail? Is it possible that God's Spirit was not done with this young man? Could the words of Jesus stay in this man's mind, replaying over and over as he walked away? Is it possible that, in the future, this young man might encounter another who would help him get closer to God? What if someone, who was also on that road when the young man asked Jesus the question about eternal life, had an encounter with this young man a few days later? That person who heard the words of Jesus and was also sad when the young man walked away. What if that person could be given the chance to speak into the life of this young man the next day? What effect might it have had on this young man?

Success is about staying true and focusing on the goal of speaking into the faith-based statement, and not about what we think the outcome should be. God's Spirit will take care of the future outcomes.

Now that we have seen these faith-based statements in action, know the DIET of brokenness, are practicing quiet time (QT), and are allowing the Holy Spirit (HS) to consume our lives, we can begin fully implementing what I call, the LOVE system into our daily lives. But to be safe, we might first need to make sure we are ready for the faith-based statements that are negative or hurtful. Once again, the scriptures give us some excellent examples.

Targeting Negative Faith-Based Statements

In Acts 26, we are given the story of Paul's arrest and abuse and then, being allowed to speak to some high government officials. When the opportunity to speak was granted to Paul, he addressed King Agrippa and an audience of high officials. Paul shared with them the story of his personal experience on the Damascus Road (Acts 9), and explained how this encounter changed his life forever. Agrippa listened intently; however, he was not impressed. The king asks, *"Do you think you can make me a Christian so quickly?"*

This is a strong faith-based statement, but in the case of Paul and King Agrippa, it is a negative statement. When we hear these types of statements, it doesn't mean that we fail. It doesn't mean that we lose sight of our goal of bringing this person one step closer to God in his or her personal transformation. We just need to rely completely on the Holy Spirit and fully trust that we may be just one part of God's bigger plan.

The apostle Paul, being our great example here, says to the King, "Whether quickly or not, I pray to God that both you and everyone here in the audience might become the same as I am, except for these chains." Paul never gave up and stuck to his goal of promoting the gospel message. His aim was to win anyone and everyone, each and every day, through each and every encounter of the day. He wasn't going to allow negativities from others to derail his goal. In fact, in this text, we are told that King Agrippa leaves and takes the other high officials with him. Paul is then led away to continue his mission and his own personal transformational journey. This encounter didn't deter Paul's mission. Paul was not stopped by the apparent rejection of the king. His intent, as always, was to bring people into a growing relationship with Jesus, and he continued with that goal in mind.

During the time of Jesus's earthly ministry, He encountered many negative and hurtful comments. For instance, while in the process of His ministry, Jesus went to the house of Matthew for a meal. Outside of the house, where Jesus and His disciples were eating, a group of Pharisees gathered. The naysayers outside spoke a clear faith-based statement of judgment and ridicule, *"Why does your teacher eat with tax collectors and sinners?"*

Jesus understood the base of this statement and the heart of those speaking it, so He gave a direct response to their question. First, He got their attention by saying, "Healthy people do not need a doctor—sick people do." Second, which was often His custom, He challenged their knowledge of scripture, by stating, "Go learn the meaning of this scripture: I want you to be merciful, I don't want your sacrifices," which the Pharisees would have known from their Old Testament study. Then, in the next sentence, He reaffirmed His mission: "For I have come to call sinners, not those who think they are already good enough" (Matthew 9:11–13 NLT).

Jesus was sent to seek and save the lost, and He stayed focused on that obligation. He was not going to lose focus because of the negative voices around Him. We need to learn from Him. If you are going to target transformation in your life and the lives of others, you must set your mind and stay the course. In the next part of this book, we will narrow the focus with more detailed information.

PART 2

Narrowing the Target

"My Father has given me authority over everything. No one really knows the Son except the Father, and no one really knows the Father except the Son and those to whom the Son chooses to reveal him." (Matthew 11:27 NLT)

CHAPTER 6

Make It Work

God does not depend on our willpower and
commitment to transform a hopeless situation.
—Henry Cloud and John Townsend,
God Will Make a Way

Setting our mind on things above is an important part of the transformation process. If we go back to the verse of Romans 12:2, Paul gives the instructions to (1) stop imitating the culture of today, (2) be transformed, and (3) by the renewing of your mind. Paul understands that, if we are going to become like Jesus, we must renew the way we think. The process will not happen otherwise. So how does that work? How do I, as a sinful person, become like an individual who never sinned? To help us with this are Paul's words written first in his letter to the church at Corinth:

> For who among men knows the thoughts of a man except the man's spirit within him? In the same way no one knows the thoughts of God except the Spirit of God. We have not received the spirit of the world but the Spirit who is from God, that we may understand what God has freely given us. This is what we speak, not in words taught us by human wisdom but in words taught by the Spirit, expressing spiritual truths in spiritual words. The man without the Spirit does not accept the things that come from the Spirit of God, for they are foolishness to him, and he cannot understand them,

because they are spiritually discerned. The spiritual man makes judgments about all things, but he himself is not subject to any man's judgment. For who has known the mind of The Lord that he may instruct him? But we have the mind of Christ. Brothers, I could not address you as spiritual but as worldly—mere infants in Christ. I gave you milk, not solid food, for you were still worldly. For since there is jealousy and quarreling among you, are you not worldly? Are you not acting like mere men?" (1 Corinthians 2:11–3:3 NIV)

"But we have the mind of Christ" (v.16b). Paul is critical of the folks in the church at Corinth for their childish actions and is telling them to grow up so he can stop delivering milk and start delivering real, spiritual meat. Paul is expressing the core issues involved in becoming like Christ. First, accept His Spirit completely, and then think like Him. That is spiritual maturity at its best. We can do that, one step at a time, from childhood to adult, with the mind of Christ.

When the group of counselors at Crucible Counseling started working on incorporating faith into the counseling offices, the directors of the program, Lori Burns and Wendy Herrberg, thought the best procedure was for me to develop some devotional materials—we called them "Integration of Faith"—that would be used at our weekly staff meetings. This overall idea was still fresh and new to us, but the concept seemed to be well-received and created a lot of interaction within the weekly meetings. Even though the idea was new to Crucible, it followed the way I was taught in pastoral counseling, so it seemed natural to share the concept. These devotions looked something like this.

Integration using David and Goliath (1 Samuel 17).
"Today the Lord will conquer you ..." (v. 46a).

Counselors may have that client who is continually pulled down by one particular giant in his or her life. The proper discussion of this Old Testament text may help motivate the client to conquer his/her giant.

Some issues from the text that might help give direction:

1. David saw Goliath different from the soldiers of Israel (v. 26).
2. David saw Goliath different than King Saul (vs. 32–33).
3. David's life experience had prepared him for the giant (vs. 34–36).
4. David knew who was in charge (vs. 37, 45–46).
5. Once Goliath was down, the rest of his army ran away and was also defeated (v.51b–52).

The challenge to the counselor, and the client, may be: is this just a childhood tale or a true story that works in today's world?

These devotions were printed on a half sheet of paper and passed to each person in attendance at the meetings. That way the counselors could read them and keep them for future reference. However, they usually created a lot of discussion in the room, and many times a counselor would relate that he or she, at that time, had a client who might benefit by hearing this particular story. The idea then developed quickly within the office. We all began to realize that we could actually help people by sharing about a particular Bible story or scriptural concept in this way.

The ongoing discussions grew and multiplied from that humble beginning. Obviously, the Crucible directors had a very good idea.

Hopefully you can see from this one example that almost any biblical story can work with this idea. The point is to listen to the person you are with. They will often give you some type of faith-based statement, and from that you can deduce which biblical concept might be the most relevant. This takes effort and listening skills on our part (more about that in chapter 8), but the potential benefit is powerful, and we must remember that our goal is transformation, moving the person one step closer to being like Christ. So, if we start with the mind of Christ, think like Him, and use His Spirit to guide us, then the success of helping your client move forward will always be there.

The next project Lori and Wendy had me work on was with Susie Howard, also on staff at East 91ˢᵗ Street Church, the church home of Crucible Counseling. Susie was not a counselor but had a lot of experience with presenting issues and motivating groups. They thought we might continue the integration idea by developing a more comprehensive Bible study concept to challenge our counselors and church staff. Together, we came up with some ideas and eventually, a title: "Thinking about Your Thinking." We listed some objectives for the project. They were:

1) Use scripture to engage one another in contemplative discussions about thinking and its relationship to sin, brokenness, transformation, and our journey toward wholeness and holiness.
2) Identify ways the world—our culture—influences us individually and corporately as the church.
3) Discern attitudes, traditions, and disciplines within the church that handicap us from being more effective in individual lives, our neighborhoods, and our culture as a whole.

4) Consider George Barna's research regarding self-described Christians' views about their spiritual journey and transformation, and how the information could be used for the benefit of us, those we serve, and the greater good of the church.

5) Value God's leadership and power in the transformation process as well as our individual role and responsibility in that process.

6) Humbly and prayerfully search the Bible and find:

    a) It to be living and active—able to judge the thoughts and attitudes of the heart (Hebrews 4:12).

    b) It is God-breathed and useful for teaching, rebuking, correcting, and training in righteousness so that the godly man or woman may be thoroughly equipped for every good work (2 Timothy 3:16).

    c) That God's promises are sweet to my taste, sweeter than honey to my mouth (Psalm 119:103).

7) Expand our familiarity with, and understanding of, scripture, and learn practical ways to integrate it into everyday problems and situations.

8) Gain a greater sense of urgency and priority to integrate biblical truths into our own lives and help others apply biblical truths in their lives.

You may note a few things from this list. We were certainly thinking "integration" not just for others, but for ourselves. We don't have to dig very deep to realize that most of us need our own personal thought processes challenged. We will not be much help to others until we come to a strong understanding of ourselves. You may also note that we used a lot of already known biblical concepts. We quote a lot of scripture. We knew we had to have these as a solid base to build upon. How else could we fight against the fallacy of thought given to us from our current cultural mind-set? We knew fighting the cultural mind-set is a huge key to the success of renewing our own minds. Also, we zeroed in on George Barna's ideas, specifically from his insights in *Maximum Faith*. Having read and discussed that book, we felt compelled to use the research and thought process that Barna had developed to help in our thinking about our thought processes. We believe these objectives came across very well. We were certainly challenged in the preparation of the studies, and each time we presented the material, it created a lot of discussion and positive feedback. It also gave me some personal direction on how to complement the targeting transformation idea.

During these studies, devotions, and interactions with the counseling team and the church staff, I was meeting at least once each month, on a one-to-one basis, with each of our resident counselors and counseling interns. These counselors and interns were also meeting with Betty Aldridge, pastor emeritus, at East 91st Street Church. Betty would focus most of her time talking about the counselors' personal lives—how they were doing with the part of themselves that might affect how they dealt with their clients or any areas of their lives that Betty may be able to speak into and help them with on a personal level. Betty was not a trained counselor as such, but she had a lot of life experience. Her expertise—hard earned after many years in the ministry—would often shine during these meetings.

It became more of my responsibility to stay with the focus of our "L-Quad" system. Because the counselors and interns met with two different people, with differing areas of focus, an overlap of conversation was promoted. Our counselors or interns may have been more prone to speak with Betty about counseling issues, or more prone to speak with me about personal issues. This was all acceptable and seemed to work quite well. I believe that the process of interacting with the different counselors and interns taught me as much as anyone else, and it's where the idea became clear that we could take the concept of integration of faith, which we were using inside the counseling room, and move the ideas out of the counseling office and into the everyday world. We also began to see that we could take the "L-Quad" and move it from a working model in the counseling session and place it nicely into the everyday world. That's when targeting transformation really began to come to life.

So now, let's take this "L-Quad" out of the counseling office and move it into a plan so that each person can share the concepts and really take advantage of the ideas in everyday life. If we can understand the thought process and the specifics, then we can use the design in everyday life. We can then use the system with each person we meet, each and every day. To accomplish this change, it seems best that we take the "L-Quad" system that we have established in the counseling office and make it more practical in day-to-day life. To do this, I like to use the acronym of LOVE (see how this compares with the "L-Quad").

> *Look Inward* (Look)
>> *Observe and Listen* (Listen)
>>> *Validate Their Value* (Learn)
>>>> *Empower through Prayer* (Leave)

This acronym makes sense to me because what we are striving for on the road map of transformation is Stop 10, Love of People (see the graph in chapter 3). So, if we acknowledge that goal, and the command of Jesus from Matthew 22:37–39 to totally love God and other people, we can center in on the word *love* and the concepts of targeting transformation.

CHAPTER 7
Look Inward

If you have an honest heart, an appetite for truth and an openness to God's Spirit, you will be gratified by the results.
—Josh McDowell and Dale Bellis, *Evidence for Joy*

This part of LOVE is totally about you. This is indeed me, looking at me, with God's help, and through His eyes. You need to be able to ask these questions:

- How am I doing on my own personal journey of transformation?
- Am I continually allowing God to break me of sin, self, and society?
- Have I come to a place where I will truly and completely surrender to God and love Him and others completely?
- We might want to consider the question that I first read in the words of Brennan Manning, "If God stops thinking about me, then God ceases to exist." Can we believe that?

These may sound like difficult questions and concepts, but they should be. These are questions that may take some time and work to get through. But that's all right. When you take the time to fully and efficiently explore your own mind, then you can know how God is currently (or has already) totally renewing your mind.

It is a challenging and interesting journey but worth the critical time and effort.

LOVE

1. **Look Inward:**
   a. Knowing me (boundaries, vision, reasons I do what I do, etc.).
   b. Romans 10:21: "All day long I open my arms to them, but they kept disobeying me and arguing with me." (NLT)

Boundaries

Each person, during this step, should consider his or her own boundaries. When it comes to interacting with other people, what are you comfortable with, and what are you not? For instance, there was a time in my ministry when I helped with an after-school program, which met at a neighboring church each Wednesday. The school system provided a bus to take the children from the school to the church, and we provided a driver and a chaperone. I was the chaperone. Each Wednesday, I went to the church, and the director of the program, along with his wife, would take me to the school so that I could leave my car at the church and have it to drive home at the end of the program. This arrangement worked well until I went to the church one day and the director and his wife were on vacation. Another lady offered to take me to the school. I said that would be fine, but we needed a chaperone. She was quite surprised and asked why. I told her that it was one of the boundaries I had set for myself. I don't ride in a car with only myself and a woman who is not my wife. This was not because I didn't trust myself, or any other woman; it was simply because people talk and gossip happens. I didn't want to subject her or myself to that possibility. This lady went immediately into another room and found a third person to ride with us; problem solved. The next week, the director was still on vacation, but I never had to restate my boundary; there were two people ready to take me to the school.

Each of you have these types of issues to think about. This one may not be an issue for you, but you need to think about what yours are. How do you feel about personal interaction with people you meet at the shopping center, or at your children's school? Are there "safe" people for you, and not so safe? It's my belief that, with the direction of God's Spirit, each person can decide and develop his or her personal boundaries within the framework of targeting transformation. You will not go wrong with God's plan in place, but you may be surprised at how He uses the plan.

Vision

Each of you also need to consider your personal vision. What is the greatest outcome you could hope for? Now think more. What is possible if God's vision exceeds yours? Proverbs 29:18 states, "Where there is no vision, the people perish; but he that keepeth the law, happy is he." (KJV) It can be helpful to read this verse in a different translation. "When people do not accept divine guidance, they run wild. But whoever obeys the law is happy." (NLT) A little different wording, but the point in the text is: you need to have a plan or you just run wild or perish. You need to consider:

1) What is my plan for my own personal transformation?
2) How do I integrate a plan to help other people with their transformation experience?

Targeting transformation is about you helping others become more like Jesus. On its own, it is an awesome vision!

Assessment

You also need to check your mind-set about the reason behind your vision. You will need to ask why you do the ministry you do. There are many good reasons, but giving thought to yours is the important part of the "Look Inward" step of the LOVE experience. Is this about you, or helping others, or bringing praise to God? I once knew a preacher who stated that he had entered the ministry because, during his high school years, he was given an opportunity to preach a message at his church. He was nervous, but somewhere in delivering that message he realized that everyone in the room had to be quiet and listen to him. He liked the power, and he liked the authority. That is when, and why, he decided to train for the ministry. This may or may not be a bad thing in and of itself; however, this is likely not the best reason to study and enter the ministry. Recognizing the truth in your own life can help each of you in many ways, and be a major benefit to those you serve and minister to.

Psalm 26:2 gives us a fine example: "Test me, O Lord, and try me, examine my heart and my mind: for your love is ever before me, and I walk continually in your truth" (NIV). Then, from Psalm 139:23, "Search me O God, and know my heart; test me and know my anxious thoughts. See if there is any offensive way in me, and lead me in the way everlasting" (NIV). You will not go wrong looking at yourself in the context of God's word and God's vision.

Preparation

Next, you need to think about the text of Romans 10:21. Much of this idea was covered in chapter 4, but it's an important part of "Looking Inward." To follow this plan, you will be asked to have conversation with, and listen to, people who may not be kind. You may find yourselves interacting with people who seem to be interested in the transformation process but may not follow through. You may also have some experiences with people who may want to use you for their own personal gain. These things are real, but can you deal with them in a loving manner? You need to always remember that God is in charge of this process and that He can, and will, develop and guide you as needed. Preacher and teacher Andy Stanley likes to say, "Do not worry about God filling your cup, just make sure you are doing the job of emptying it." You have a job to do. People need you to hold out your hands to them, and you can. You need to do the job each day of emptying whatever God has given you for that day. That's your part of the responsibility. He will follow through with His part.

I used to help with Little League baseball teams. I would tell the kids that they would play in the games the same way they played in practice. Some of the players didn't always go for the advice, however. They wanted to take it easy in practice and then simply show up and play well during the games. That doesn't work in Little League, and it won't work in this process of ministry through targeting transformation. You have to be willing to empty your cup every day.

The words of Jesus in John 14:1 sum up this step for me: "Don't be troubled. You trust God, now trust me" (NLT). Now, move on in a positive manner with boundaries, vision, and personal preparation in place.

CHAPTER 8
Observe and Listen

If the Christian life is simply a matter of doing our best, there was no need for God to send the Holy Spirit to help us.
—Charles Stanley, *The Wonderful Spirit-Filled Life*

Most of us need to be better at observing the people around us. Almost every day we encounter people on the street, at our school, in the workplace, and even in our families who live life around us, and we pay no attention to them. Too many days we don't even recognize their existence, but we should. I know there are those gifted individuals who have such a discerning spirit that they can detect a broken heart from across the stadium of an NFL football game and then find a way to meet the struggling soul, giving comfort and encouragement. But these folks are few. Most of us are too busy doing our own thing to take the time to give so much as a look toward the others we're around daily.

LOVE
2. **O**bserve and Listen:
    a. Focus on the actions and words of others, their phrases, and their faith-based ideas.
    b. When do I hear God whisper?

This part of LOVE is about focusing on the actions and words of other people. If you work at it, people will give you clues about how they are doing with life through their observable actions. Facial expressions, eye contact (or lack thereof), the way their eyes light up when they talk about certain subjects, and the way they move are all outward indicators of how and what a person is feeling on the inside. In the targeting transformation model, think about these actions, and work at observing how other people send you signals through their actions. Then you can place your personal observations alongside the words they say. You can observe and listen.

Listening

The world today is losing the art of listening. We can put headphones in while we text on our phone, and at the same time, be watching a TV or computer screen while driving down the road. Though it may be a bit of an exaggeration, we are in a time of unlimited opportunities for communication, and we are losing the desire to talk to other people face-to-face. We need this part of the LOVE system.

The story about Elijah in chapter 4 was given to help you find a time and place where you can hear God whisper. I put this biblical account within the content of the DIET formula of brokenness because I believe it is a must for people who want to stay in the ministry. I place it here in LOVE because, again, it is most important. This has some clear reference to the "Look Inward" and will also have a place in "Validate their Value," the next step of LOVE. God must be heard quietly and directly. If you've lost that quiet time, or if you've never had it, now might be the time to find it. When you get committed to targeting transformation, it is imperative that you hear what people are saying, and I believe that idea starts with listening to God and allowing Him to give you a clear direction and discernment. This all begins with hearing Him. You don't have to wait until you are fearful and depressed, as Elijah did.

There is a humorous story about a preacher who came home from work on Friday evening. It was late, and he had had a long and very busy week. His mind was on resting and enjoying a nice Saturday breakfast at home with his wife and kids, whom he hadn't seen very much during the week. When he walked through the door at home, his wife was fixing him a light meal. The children were already in bed, and his wife was equally tired. She greeted her husband and said, "Dear, I have been so busy all day with the kids that I have not had time to go to the grocery. We need a loaf of bread for our Saturday breakfast. Would you please go get one before you sit down?"

The husband shook his head yes and headed back toward the door. Then, the wife said, "Sweetie, if they have eggs, get a dozen." He nodded his affirmation before leaving. Shortly thereafter, the husband returned home with twelve loaves of bread.

We get busy. We get fixated on one specific task, or we are juggling so many tasks at once that we fail to completely hear the conversations around us. Or we think we heard the words correctly only to find out we didn't because we didn't really listen. In the previous story about the preacher, they ended up with plenty of bread for Saturday breakfast, but no eggs.

Often in helping couples with their communication skills, I share an activity called active or reflective listening. The couple sits in chairs facing each other; they maintain eye contact and speak directly to each other. First, the husband or wife will speak to his or her spouse. This needs to be just a few sentences, nothing too long. Second, the other will repeat the same words back to the first person. They can use the exact words, or at the very least, a close paraphrasing of the words they heard. Third, the first person will agree and say the same words back again to his or her spouse. This all seems redundant, but it works well in achieving proper communication. The success is known because the person who spoke first now understands that he or she was heard by the second person, and the second person knows the first also heard and understood the same words. Now, both parties know they have each heard the same words. This is where proper communication starts, by looking at the person, watching his or her facial expressions, and *listening*.

During these times of communication with couples, we also look at and discuss a list of blocks to listening. I was given these in a marriage mentoring folder from Dr. Doug Spears while at Cincinnati Christian University in 1995. When you take the time to read each of the blocks and think about them, you will likely realize that you fall prey to these blocks many times throughout the day. Sometimes it's a habit you have unintentionally acquired, or you might use these blocks so you don't have to listen. That might be because you're too busy, or merely not interested in the story or information you're hearing. When you recognize one or more of these blocks, you can choose to continue them, or you can choose to find ways of listening and changing some bad habits.

Blocks to Listening

1) *Comparing*: You're trying to assess who is smarter, more competent, more emotionally stable, who has suffered more. It is difficult to listen when you're busy seeing if you measure up.

2) *Mind Reading*: You're not paying attention to what another says; rather you're trying to figure out what the other person is *really* thinking. The mind reader looks for intonations and subtle cues and relies heavily on intuitions, hunches, and vague misgivings.

3) *Filtering*: You pay attention only to that which is important to you. Sometimes you quit listening when you find out there is no real *serious* problem. You may also "not hear" negative, critical, or unpleasant things.

4) *Rehearsing*: You can't listen well when you are carefully preparing your next comment. You *look* interested, but your mind is on your own agenda.

5) *Judging*: This is essentially hypercritical evaluations based on prejudgment. Judgment of discernment should only be made after careful reflection of the communication.

6) *Dreaming*: As you listen, something someone says triggers a chain of thoughts regarding issues unrelated to the present. This often happens when one is feeling bored or anxious, or when there is little commitment to the one speaking.

7) *Identifying*: You refer everything a person tells you back to your own experience. The focus is really upon yourself and your own need to be heard.

8) *Advising*: You have the solution that will solve the problem. With a little information you can "fix it." You easily miss the feelings and the pain communicated.

9) *Sparring*: Your desire is to argue and debate. You focus on that which you disagree about. One type of sparring is the put-down.

10) *Being Right*: You can't listen openly because you have to protect yourself from being wrong.

11) *Derailing*: You suddenly change the subject because you're bored or uncomfortable with the topic. One way to derail is to continually respond with a joke or quip.

12) *Placating*: You want people to like you, so you agree with most anything that is said.

> **Note**: Self-awareness is crucial to overcome listening blocks! The problem with the above listening blocks is oneself getting in the way.

Observation

When the active listening exercise and the blocks to listening are talked about with couples, we usually get to a place where the couple realizes that there is more than one thought behind the few sentences shared together. For instance, say the wife asks the husband, "Do you think we can paint the garage this Saturday?"

The husband may not want to hear this suggestion, or he may just be busy on Saturday. The wife may know both of these things, but what if the question the wife really is asking sounds more like this: "Can we please spend some time together this weekend?"

That becomes a different matter. It is not about paint or the garage. It is about building, strengthening, or rebuilding their relationship.

Targeting transformation is about the same thing. You may think you are going to listen for some faith-based wording from a person. However, in reality, you are looking to build a relationship with that person. But more importantly, you are seeking to find an opportunity for their relationship with Jesus Christ to grow. That is not about some temporary wording; it is about eternal relationships. These relationships are well worth your effort. This is not about us. There needs to be an understanding that you are dedicating your ears to hear for God's glory. This may be looked at as your act of sharing God's grace with others, by helping bring them closer to Christ. As the writer of Hebrews 13:16 states, "And do not forget to do good and to share with others, for with such sacrifices God is pleased" (NIV).

You hear faith-based statements every day. Most of the time you are simply not listening for them, or you don't have a reason to do anything with them unless your target is transformation of the person you are listening to. When you review the scriptures and see the faith-based statements that Jesus heard (we looked at some of these in chapter 5) we see that He must have been paying attention to the words people said. Then, His actions often followed those statements. What do you do when you hear these types of statements? Are you willing to step into them? Are you willing to make the sacrifice necessary to listen?

If I'm shopping and the store worker who is checking out my items asks, "How is your day, sir?" that's pretty much a neutral question, and the employee has been trained to ask it. If I comment with, "Not bad. How is yours?" it's still normal, everyday communication. We then may go about our transaction and not have another word. Normal, but not in targeting transformation. In targeting transformation, I am seeking to build a relationship with that person. I must not be too busy for deeper conversation. I must not be so wrapped up in my own needs that I stop thinking about helping that person get one step closer to Jesus. In the future, I may look for that employee again. We may interact with more words the next time and that person may speak some faith-based statement that can act as a starting point.

For instance, what if that same employee, the next time I pass through his checkout, says, "How are you, sir?" and I say, "Great, how are you?" And he responds with, "Not that good. My mom is in the hospital, and I'm worried about her." I don't want to block this statement, so I repeat it. "So your mom is in the hospital, and you're worried?" This person knows I heard. That is a big step, especially in the busyness of our average checkout lane. This employee may have shared that personal information to others who have come through the checkout line, maybe not, but now it has been said to me. I may need to discern some issues here, but I hope to proceed with a prayer and a belief that God's Spirit will be in charge. This employee has not yet given me a faith-based statement, but he knows I am listening. No headphones, no phone in my face—just ears that want to hear. In our world today, that's huge. I just need to make sure it's for the right reasons. But to achieve anything more, I need to listen and observe.

CHAPTER 9
Validate Their Value

Words can encourage, discourage, or do nothing.
—Larry Crabb, *Encouragement: The Key to Caring*

People need to know that they have value. If we understand how much love God has for each and every person, and then validate and share that wisdom with others, we will be highly successful in this area of LOVE, both in the short-term and the long-term.

LOVE

3. Validate their value:
   a. Short-term understanding and long-term strategy of showing value to other people
   b. Grow in wisdom
   c. Know my environment

Short-Term and Long-Term

More than once, I've told preachers who are starting a new ministry that, in their first year, they should do nothing except love people and preach the gospel. Then, again in the second year, they should love people and preach the gospel, while possibly suggesting a few ideas for change within the church. The third year they should continue to love people and preach the gospel while becoming more directed in making changes in the congregation. Only after the church knows you love them, and they understand more about the gospel message, will they be ready to make necessary changes. Then, in the future, never forget to love people and preach the gospel. If you take the time to show folks that you love and value them, you will then learn how to speak into their lives, and they will be ready to listen.

This directive was given to me years ago as I started a preaching ministry position at a church in which the two preachers before me had each been in the position for only a short time. In the previous three years, this church had seen two ministers come and go. Why would I be any different? Short-term understanding and long-term strategy is sound, and though it may seem a bit overstated in some cases, it works well in most. The short-term teaches folks how to accept love and how to be loved. That is also the long-term strategy because it will bring people to Christ (love folks, preach the gospel).

In the LOVE strategy, short-term is day-to-day, person to person. By your efforts, you will bless many people, some just by conversation or pausing long enough to observe and listen to them. You won't be focused on bringing people to faith in Christ, although that can happen because it certainly is reaching the goal of bringing them one step closer to Jesus. With this idea, you might need to remember the words of Jesus in what we label the Great Commission from Matthew 28:19-20.

> Therefore, go and make disciples of all the nations, baptizing them in the name of the Father and the Son and the Holy Spirit. Teach these new disciples to obey all the commands I have given you. And be sure of this: I am with you always, even to the end of the age. (NLT)

Functioning today as His disciples, you need to be in obedience of these words. "Go," from my understanding and training, is translated to the effect of as you go through life, not after you get somewhere in life. To put the concept in everyday terms, you are to make disciples while you proceed down the road of everyday life. It's not that you leave from point A and you start making disciples only after you've arrived at point B. In fact, you may be offered the opportunity of speaking to people and winning them to Christ while you are traveling from point A to point B or anywhere in between. Then you are given the command of continuing to teach them to obey His commands, which, in part, is "Follow Me," or "Be like Me." That's where transformation works. This is best-explained in the poem from *Streams in the Desert* devotional journal.

> Follow Me, and I will make you ...
> Make you speak My words with power,
> Make you channels of My mercy,
> Make you helpful every hour.
> Follow Me, and I will make you ...
> Make you what you cannot be,
> Make you loving, trustful, godly,
> Make you even like to Me.[4]

Transformation is in the short-term, but it also becomes the long-term. When you bring people to Christ, they follow Him and become like Him, and He makes them so many things. Some of these things happen in this world, some in the next. Your part seems to be focused in this world. He will take care of the next.

Growth
You also need to apply this in the area of personal growth. If you are (1) going to observe and listen to people, (2) hear some form

---

[4] Mrs. Charles Cowman, *Streams in the Desert: A Daily Devotional Journal* (Uhrichsville, OH: Barbour Publishing, Inc., 1965), March 15.

of faith-based statement, and (3) learn how to share some biblical concept, scripture thought, or story, you need to have a good bit of biblical knowledge. There seems to be no better way of doing this than reading and studying the scriptures yourself. Author Greg Ogden speaks into this area in a book titled *Transforming Discipleship,* where he writes,

> Most potential disciples have bits and pieces of Christian teaching interspersed with worldviews from contemporary culture. This usually means that people have disconnected pieces of knowledge, much like puzzle pieces, but people have never put the pieces together to see the big picture of the Christian life.[5]

Ogden understands the challenge in today's world. We learn so much from worldly conversation that is contrary to scripture, but we believe it is scripture. Most of us could use much more biblical understanding and clarity. If you continue to learn about Jesus, He will continue to show you ways of using this knowledge. This learning will help you put all the puzzle pieces together correctly. As my friend Pastor Matt Smith likes to say, "If you want to know about Jesus, read about Jesus. If you want to understand Jesus, study Jesus."

This becomes so important in the targeting transformation process because most of the people we encounter in this life have the same issue Greg Ogden points out (as do most of us). Their knowledge of scripture is so mixed with a current worldview. We often hear people say, "The Bible says ..." when in fact, the Bible doesn't say that at all. You will be much more successful throughout this process if you have the correct biblical knowledge to share. But please, don't be hindered by any excuse that says

---

[5] Greg Ogden, *Transforming Discipleship* (Downers Grove: InterVarsity Press, 2003), 164.

you don't know the Bible well enough. You will certainly do well to learn as you go; on-the-job training is acceptable here. In fact, there are many intelligent biblical scholars who do not work well in the area of one-on-one interactions and relationships. You might need to remember the old adage: *"Knowledge puffs up, love lifts up."*

Knowledge comes from study, but wisdom—the life details about how to use that knowledge—comes from God. If you allow yourself to observe and learn from Him (love other people) and apply the biblical concepts through the power of His Spirit, then you should have no fear of failure on your part, or His.

Environment

You also need to understand your environment. Who are the people you are most likely to be meeting? I was sharing this idea at a conference, and one of the people in the audience shared a great story about understanding the people in your environment. This man and his wife were serving a church in Indiana. His wife was from a small town, and the man said that she'd never met a stranger. She talked to every person she met as though they had known each other all their lives. However, the husband was from New York City. On a trip to visit family in New York, the wife was being herself and talking to everyone she saw on the street. Her actions didn't go over well. People avoided her. They were afraid of her and gave her dirty looks. Although this may seem like a good way to validate and show value to other people, the small Midwest idea of friendliness did not translate the same way in downtown New York City. The wife became upset and asked her husband what was wrong. He told her, "You're in a different environment. People here don't understand why you're acting this way." She had to take time to learn her new environment.

The late college professor and author Dr. Joe Ellis wrote a

very helpful book entitled *The Church On Purpose*. In this work, he speaks about our need to understand the people we will minister to.

> Jesus and all He represented were alien to the world as it had become because of sin. Yet He entered the culture of first-century Palestine, lived in the homes, wore the clothing, ate the food, spoke the language, and partook of the daily life of the people. The Word was clothed in the flesh *and culture* of man in order to reconcile men to God. He was *in* culture, yet alien to it, and used culture to relate to human beings. His uniqueness was clothed in the familiar and the understandable. This relationship is delicate. Christianity is alien to the world but must exist in and make use of the cultures of the world for God's purposes.
>
> If the church is to evangelize effectively, it must identify with the culture around it. It must be perceived as understanding and caring about the people around it – how they think and feel, where they hurt, and what they need. The church should be a living demonstration of how Christianity works in a given culture, how people live God's way and do His work in *this* set of circumstances.[6]

You will need to know the people you are living and working with, and then, you will be much better prepared to develop and respond encouragingly to them. This response will then fit into their understanding of scriptural truth. If you know the culture, then you know the people.

You might be helped by one of my favorite authors, Dr. David Faust, who wrote a book on evangelism called *Taking Truth Next*

---

[6] Joe Ellis, *The Church on Purpose: Keys to Effective Church Leadership* (Cincinnati: Standard Publishing, 1982), 170–71.

Door. In this book, Dr. Faust speaks at some length about how our culture is changing. He speaks about things like modernism, post-modernism, and pluralism. These are all important concepts to help you understand our culture. Some see these trends as totally negative for us in the church, while some recognize that these people groups and a changing culture are mostly just misguided souls who need more clarity and direction on their way to finding the right path. Dr. Faust, in his optimistic nature, shares some good news that can help us open many doors of communication. He writes,

> Today's spiritual curiosity may be misguided, but it is a good thing. Many are recognizing and abandoning the hollow, empty religious traditions and stubborn denominational loyalties that have held sway in our culture for decades. Isn't it good that most of our neighbors still believe God answers prayer, and that they're questioning the rationalism and naturalism that long have held Western culture in their grip?

> Isn't it encouraging to see that people still hunger for genuine Christian love? Our love must be demonstrated in real life. Can we host effective small groups in our homes, build one-on-one friendships with seekers, and create mentoring programs in which older Christians or successfully married couples take younger people under their wings and support them with love and kindness? Can we address the current fascination with art through coffee houses, drama presentations, and quality music? Can we find ways to bring more Christian input into the media?

> Can we learn to communicate cross-culturally and reach across ethnic lines to build bridges for the gospel? Can we develop preaching and teaching styles that include thought–provoking stories and allow for discussion,

interaction and feedback? Can we develop evangelism methods that build trust over time instead of demanding immediate decisions? Can we learn not only to answer the question, "Is there a God?" but also explain *"Which God?"*[7]

I believe that we have relationships, discussions, and interactions that can create personal feedback and positive results. I believe that we can speak to the culture of today, as individuals, and through the feedback we receive from these individuals, we can share life in a way that brings them closer to being like Christ. We do not have to demand immediate results; we just have to stay faithful to the plan and continue to realize that each and every person has great value in the eyes of the God whom we all serve.

When you work this plan of interacting with other people, you may make mistakes, but that is no reason to feel defeated. You will have to stay with it. If you're not successful the first time, then adjust your plan so that it will work better in the current culture or situation that you are in. You may need to find another person, or group of people, that you can speak with about learning more in regard to helping others with their transformation. You may need wise individuals to give some personal feedback in this area.

You may also be encouraged by some thoughts from Dr. Henry Cloud, which are written in his book *Necessary Endings*.

> Wise people learn from experience and make adjustments... The person who ultimately does well is the one who can learn from his own experience or the experience of others, make that learning a part of himself, and then deliver results from that experience base.[8]

---

[7] David Faust, *Taking Truth Next Door* (Cincinnati: Standard Publishing, 1999), 38.

[8] Henry Cloud, *Necessary Endings* (New York: HarperCollins, 2010), 126–27.

As well, Dr. Cloud goes on to list some traits of wise people. Here are a few:

Traits of Wise Persons:

➢ When you give them feedback, they listen, take it in, and adjust their behavior accordingly.

➢ When you give them feedback, they embrace it positively. They say things like, "Thank you for telling me that. It helps me to know I came across that way."

➢ They own their performance, problems, and issues and take responsibility for them without excuses or blame.

➢ Your relationship is strengthened as a result of giving them feedback.

➢ They empathize and express concern about the results of their behavior on others.

➢ They do not allow problems that have been addressed to turn into patterns.[9]

All of this takes work and effort. It takes short-term and long-term understanding, it takes growing in knowledge and wisdom, and it takes a basic understanding of the people we encounter in our environment. It may also take great effort in finding people you can rely on to give you some positive feedback; however, when targeting transformation is active in your life, it will change your life, and the process will change the lives of those you touch.

---

[9] Cloud, *Necessary Endings*, 129–30.

CHAPTER 10

Empower through Prayer

The least little remembrance will always be acceptable
to Him. You need not cry very loud.
—Brother Lawrence, *The Practice of the Presence of God*

You do a lot of things with your time. You may have a demanding job, kids, relatives that need your attention, or church activities that are important. So only you can ask yourself to take the time to participate in this part of the LOVE process. But even as you look at the major time consumers in your life, there is probably some extra time for important activities—for example, lifting others up to the Lord in prayer. It is very possible, in the targeting transformation actions, that most of the people you interact with during the day will be family members, friends, or coworkers. Who better to help these uniquely placed people than you? Who better to lift before the Lord, to pour into their lives, and to seek His guidance for them? Who better to encourage before the Lord than the very ones you are already living life with? What joy will you feel when you see these people, already placed in your life, grow closer to Christ?

LOVE

4. **Empower through prayer:**
   a. I need to prayerfully reflect on all the above (Look Inward, Observe and Listen, and Validate Their Value).
   b. Most specifically, each and every person that I meet during the day and what happens during those encounters.

Prayer is a major key to success in targeting transformation. In this area of LOVE, you are being asked to pause, at some point in your day, and mentally review each person you talked to during your day. You can step before the Lord and have a quiet time of review and discussion about how you handled each interaction during your day. This again takes time, effort, and work, but placed into action it can become a very natural part of the process. There is nothing more empowering to do for another person than to bring him or her before the influence of God via the medium of prayer.

Reflect

In my early years of working as a full-time minister and pastor, I read two books that changed my focus on how I spent my time. One was *Too Busy Not to Pray* by Bill Hybels, and the other was *No God but God* by Os Guinness. Bill Hybels wrote from the perspective of a busy pastor and senior minister at Willow Creek Community Church near Chicago. This mega church and all its activities could have taken all of Hybels's time. But in the book, he states that the most important thing he did every day was pray; he was too busy not to. Hybels knew he needed God's voice and direction in his decision-making, and he accepted that clearly.

Os Guinness reached out and challenged me with his words about idolatry. He asked the question: What is it that we put before God? Anything that we do, say, have, feel, touch, or dream about can become an idol that takes us away from our worship of

God. I had to consider that question in my own life, more than once, when I first read his book. I still do.

What is important to God? That becomes the real question. Transformation is so vital in our walk with Jesus that we must give it the time and place of highest calling. Then to be able to speak into another person's life and help with their transformation journey is amazing beyond words. So, to come before the Lord at some point each day and retrace our steps with Him is a very cool, sometimes eye-opening experience as His Spirit uncovers things you might have missed at the time. Sometimes this time of reflection will bring peace in knowing you spoke into a person's life, with God's assent and direction, and from then on God will take that interaction and process it His way. Your part may be complete, at least for that day, and that time, for that person. The verse that speaks clearly to me on this subject is 1 John 5:21, "Dear children, keep away from anything that might take God's place in your hearts." (NLT)

Your worldly stuff will get in the way. Your family will sometimes take priority. Your job will often call when you don't want to answer. Your church family will need you to serve at times that aren't to your liking. You will need to find the balance. You will have to work within that balance, and the priorities of life, just as everyone else has to work the same types of issues out in their lives. How God prompts you to continue will be between you and Him.

Using the LOVE step of "Empowering through Prayer" is meant to focus you on people, faces, conversations, and individual words that happened during the day. You don't just walk away from a person when the conversation is finished. You let God linger in it, mold the wording in it, ruminate, and mature the memory of each conversation as you remember it and as He enlightens your memory. You learn from His Spirit, you lean on

His Spirit, and you are humbled by His Spirit. This learning, leaning, and humbling will directly affect your transformation as well as those you encounter daily.

Each and Every Person

Going back to the conversation I might have at the store checkout (chapter 8), the employee and I shared only a few words of conversation. Because of the employee's words, I might truly be interested in how the employee's mother is doing in the hospital, but that is not my focus. My focus is on the individual with whom I now have direct interaction: this one employee. This is solely about one employee, at one store, on this one day. I take to God that one face-to-face interaction. My prayer is for that one person and it is specific: transformation. This is empowering. I may not know the name of the employee, but it doesn't matter. God knows him or her by name, just as He knows mine. So my prayer to the Creator of the universe, through the name of Jesus, is to bring this one person before God and ask Him to bring him or her closer to Jesus. How will, or might, God do that? I do not know. My job in targeting transformation, at this stage, is to lift up that person. What better way is there to bring a person closer to Christ than to lift them up in prayer? To have them come before The Lord is a mighty thing. What if you are the only one doing so for this one person, this one day, at this one time?

This process will broaden your awareness of each conversation you have during the day. You will be surprised at how God broadens your perspective on day-to-day conversations. He will show you in prayer the way one conversation connects to a different conversation you had that day, or on a different day. You will grow in this process. You will begin to look at your conversations during the day with a different point of view, knowing that you are going to remember each conversation in prayer later that day.

In so doing, you will grow closer to Christ—you will grow in your transformation.

When I started the position at Crucible Counseling, their office was sixty miles from my house. That seventy to ninety-minute drive (depending on time of day and traffic) was long. I was used to a fifteen-minute commute, but the directors at Crucible and I had agreed on only two days a week. That seemed to make it tolerable, since I had other commitments closer to home on the other days. However, after several months, the two days turned into four, and then into full-time. Then, each week, I had a lot of driving time.

Fortunately, my prayer time began to fill this space during my drive. I insisted (to myself) that nothing be allowed to sit on the passenger seat of my car. This became my time to have conversation with Jesus. The seat next to me was His. It was just the two of us spending at least two hours a day in conversation. It was easy to turn on the radio, especially in the morning, to catch the local traffic issues, or in the evenings just to unwind, but that would ruin our special time. It would have been acceptable to talk on the phone; however, after a while, it became natural for me to speak to the Lord. While I navigated the drive into the church in the mornings, we had talks about each person I was meeting that day. On the way home, we would converse about each person I had talked with during the day. These were not audible, out-loud conversations, although I did speak aloud many times. I can say I never heard Jesus speak to me in the same manner another person sitting in the passenger seat would, but I heard Him, clearly and on many occasions. More than once, I was challenged or frustrated by a particular situation and an understanding came into my spirit, in that car, that was an answer to a prayer, and I gave God praise with joy.

When that counseling position ended, I was sad to lose my

personal time with the Lord. I had grown used to the special time, and I then had to find a new time in my schedule to replace it. There is always this quality time for you and God; you just have to find it. Using that time is what the LOVE step of "Empower through Prayer" is all about.

PART 3

Zeroing in on the Target

Then Jesus said, "Come to me, all of you who are weary and carry heavy burdens…" (Matthew 11:28-30 NLT)

CHAPTER 11
Use the Map

Let me tell you that God, who began a good work in
you, is not about to stop now.
—Jim Cymbala and Dean Merrill, *Fresh Faith*.

When I went with my wife and son to Rocky Mountain National Park in 1990, we didn't plan on riding horses to Odessa Lake, one of the highest elevated lakes in the continental United States. But this turned out to be a marvelous adventure. The day we signed up we were told to pack a sack lunch, bring it with us the next day, and be at the Glacier Creek Stables ready to ride at 7:30 a.m. We were prepared and there on time, anticipating the day, but we did not understand how steep of a climb it was to the top. Each of us was first introduced to the horse we were to ride for the day. We were told to trust our horse, because each one had made the climb several times. In the moment, we did not understand the full depth of that bit of instruction, but we soon would.

During the first part of our ride, the terrain was flat and was largely uneventful. We were still close to the stable and getting used to our horses, as well as them to us. Our guide was a college student who was familiar with the area, but she was only working at the stable during the summer break. She seemed to be under the impression that our family would work out any struggles we had, and we would figure out what we needed to do. Perhaps it was clear to her that we were more or less at home in the saddle, and there were others on the trip who had never seen the world from the back of a horse. They clearly needed more personal assistance, and she spent most of her time with them.

However, the path soon changed, and we started our journey up the mountain, the elevation increasing rapidly. The Rocky Mountains can be steep, and to reach our destination we were forced to move up quickly in elevation. Even though the scenery was incredible and beautiful to admire, I kept thinking about the ride back down. To me, a flatlander from the Midwest, this trail was too steep to ride the same way back down. Surely there would be another way on the return trip back to the stable, some type of switchback trail or something. I was wrong. The path we took up was also the path down, and the downward journey took more faith in my horse than going up; however, the time at the top was worth it. Lunch at the lake was almost spiritual. It seemed that we talked in whispers. We were at the elevation where the trees stopped and the rocks took over. The lake looked like a glass tabletop, and the blue spruce pines swayed in peaceful reverence. The twisted, weatherworn Krummholz trees were so much more noble and majestic in person than any picture I'd ever seen of them. The elevation wasn't the only thing that was taking my breath away—the environment was awesome in every way! Our panoramic view made even the flavor of peanut butter and jelly sandwiches taste like a gourmet meal. We wanted to stay, but as soon as we ate, it was time to mount for our descent. The horses had a schedule to keep, and the guide knew it. Besides, this was not our destination in life. When we got back down to our car, we had to make the day-long drive home; there was work to do.

Most of us like vacations, but most of us have work to do. What if targeting transformation is added to that to-do list? Can it get done? Can you fit it in? The good thing about this concept is that it should not be just another thing to do. It should be the thing you do while you do those other things on your daily to-do list. If this goal of being determined to work with God to transform ourselves is being sought after, then how much more effort is it to help others along your journey? Can you look back on great memories of where you've been, and can those memories motivate you to continue the climb? The view at the top of this transformation mountain is fantastic, but it will be one step better if you help others achieve that same view.

I believe that, for us as the church to achieve any measurable success toward this target of transformation, our goals will need to be accomplished through the church. That being said, the church in today's world is changing. I don't believe that most people today are happy or fulfilled by attending a 10:30 Sunday morning worship; however, some settle for it, because it is easy and short. Most believers today don't attend the normal, traditional worship service and then rejoice about their growth or personal transformation. Today's churches come in any number of shapes and sizes. Today's church attendees are asked to participate in many different programs, which their church sells and promote. These programs are designed to fit the goals their church hopes to accomplish. Targeting transformation is not a program. It is a concept that can permeate each and every program in the church. It is an idea that can change the dynamic of each program and each person in your congregation. This idea can be used in conservative, traditional churches or new, revolutionary congregations. Your traditions and your church's future do not change this exciting concept. But it can, and will, grow the individuals within your church, and therefore, the entire church. To accomplish this, you will need a correct, up-to-date map.

When my family first explored the beauty of God's creation at Rocky Mountain National Park, we had no intention of riding.

We saw the horses and the stable, so we stopped and asked for information. The workers at the stable were busy. Riders were coming and going. So they gave us a brochure with information and told us that what we needed to know was in that brochure and also on a sign at the office.

The brochure listed several different riding options, length of rides, departure times, and costs. When we asked for clarification about which ride we should take, the general answer was that they were all good and we just needed to think about how much time we had, how experienced we were, and what we wanted to do. We had to figure it out on our own.

A lot of our church signs help people in the same way. Our church web page, our newsletters, and our Sunday bulletins give a lot of information and options, and if people ask which they should choose, we often give a similar answer. "It's totally up to you. How much time do you have? How much experience do you have?" For those new to the church, this is often not much help, and they are often left to figure it out on their own. How does knowing this information help people with their transformation journey?

These comments may seem a bit negative toward the church as a whole. I hope instead that they can be a challenge. Serving as a minister and pastor for many years, it seemed like my biggest challenge was often to help people navigate the church. My job, from my perspective, and I think a biblical slant, was to "win the lost and encourage the saints." That takes on a lot of different forms. My job, from a more direct biblical perspective, was the great commission from Jesus (Matthew 28:19–20). However, I worked very hard at winning folks to Christ, but was most often struggling with how to get them properly integrated into the church family. We often had to ask newcomers to attend a Bible study or Sunday school class that was made up of people who had been in the church for twenty or thirty years. It was usually intimidating and awkward for the new member. We tried to have Christian apologetics or Christian life skills classes for new members, which sometimes were well attended, but most of the time we had as many long-time members there as new members. We always seemed to find it difficult to take people fresh from the waters of baptism and stay with them through the growing process of living the Christian life. The road up the mountain of Christian living was too steep, too curvy, too dark, and too uncertain. There was often no safe place.

I know, from churches and information printed by hard-working pastors and ministers, that a great deal of effort is placed on areas of discipleship and Christian growth within our churches. In my experience, most of these programs center around some type of foundations class for new members, or a group or discipleship class. There are also churches who are blessed with a specific minister who has the title of discipleship minister. One of my favorites (because I have used it the most) is a discipleship plan that uses a workbook format in which one person sets a time to meet with one or two other people, and together, they work through the information in the workbook. Then, each person who completes the workbook, after a period of several weeks, finds another person or two and works through the information with them. With this program, you can make disciples of your entire city in less than three years. Very good, but what then?

Do the people who complete these programs get a diploma that states they are true disciples? I believe this is where targeting transformation comes into effect. I most certainly don't want to take away from any program that is working, but most programs do not work for the same individual long-term. Most of these programs are as much about a basic Bible study, or the history of the church, as they are about becoming more like Jesus. Targeting transformation is not a program in itself; it is a system that can work with any, and all, existing programs and at the same time multiply the efforts of that program. Targeting transformation will take individuals beyond the basic studying of the Bible and church history and into a realm of truly living the command of Jesus to love God and others. However, we need to be willing to follow the new map.

Using the New Map

I now believe that if we teach the church family how to target transformation, this navigation within the church can be different, because now we have a map. The graph in chapter 3 can help give direction and clarity; we can bring people into the church family and help them by talking about transformation. We can share with them what this process looks like, what the objectives are, and how the church can help. Each person will take a different road, and that's okay, but our goal is the same: be like Jesus. We can then allow the new members, who have come from Stop 4 to Stop 5 to seek their place in the safety of the church until they are ready to take the next step, Stop 6. We can also challenge our longtime members with this map. We can ask about how God is challenging them to move into Stop 6, and how are they doing with the brokenness in Stop 7. We now can look at this journey in a new and fresh light. This can be a powerful help for church members who may have been stuck for years in the easy and safe life of church involvement and are missing out on the wonderful climb to the top of the mountain, where they will find peace and a beauty more majestic than they have ever experienced before. This Brokenness Stop (7) will be a key in our forward movement. It is the most difficult part of the climb because it is the stop that we in the church must learn to deal with, and the part that we must learn to help other believers into and through. But who will help them?

During our ride up the mountain trail, we came to a river. The water was just over knee deep on the horses, but it was moving rapidly and was very loud. Our guide went through the water first, and everyone else followed except for one boy, who looked to be about twelve or thirteen years old. His horse would not step into the water. My family waited for him as the guide yelled directions from across the river. The boy was clearly nervous, and the horse was getting a little out of control. It soon became clear that they both needed help. I rode up to the boy and told him I was going to take the lead rope from his saddle horn and lead him across the river. I told him that when he got to the edge of the water, he needed to spur his horse so that the animal understood that they were going through the water to the other side. I looped the lead rope around my saddle horn and led the boy and his horse to the edge of the water. This time his horse did not hesitate, and we went across the river safely. That one boy just needed a little help to show him the way.

I believe the same thing happens in transformation. Who do we have to guide us? I'm not talking about biblical guides like reading about Jesus and doing what He did. I'm talking about one-to-one, face-to-face, eye-to-eye, person-to-person interactions of encouragement and leading. We need other people who know something about this transformation journey who can share the path, or show us the trail. Even though the journey, for each person, will be different in many ways, having another person's knowledge and understanding will be most helpful.

One of the most difficult stops on the transformation road map is Stop 7, Brokenness. We touched on this idea in chapter 3, but in Barna's book *Maximum Faith* he spends a great deal of time with this stop. Barna relays this information about that stop:

As believers dive into this new commitment, God meets them head-on with the realization that they are still too self-reliant and have never fully come to grips with the implications of their sin. Confession is one thing; feeling and dealing with the weight of what the confessed sins have done to their relationship with a holy and loving God is another. Some people have experienced a degree of brokenness, addressing their sin but not their independence, so God endeavors to show them the ravages of self-reliance.

So God takes them through a time of in-your-face confrontation. Serious believers finally reach a state of brokenness, which prepares them for the glorious healing and reconstruction that God has in mind for them. This takes them beyond merely accepting the offer of salvation to the experience of authentic, shared love and a truly purposeful life. But this brokenness only comes after much reflection and meditation, sorrow and remorse, realistic, self-evaluation, talking and listening to God, and coming to the end of self as the 'go to' person in all situations. This is largely about realigning our spirit with God's.[10]

"Realigning our spirit with God's"? Going through the pain of self-evaluation, remorse, sorrow, and meditation? Who wants to do all that work? That may be a big reason why only 3 percent of the people in Barna's survey were actually on this stop, and why so few get past it. It's difficult, but look again at the reward for accomplishing this part of the journey. Those who stay on this trail go beyond just an offer of salvation and can now experience authentic shared love (you and God) and a truly purposeful life. Sometimes, to get to the top of the mountain of transformation, you must simply saddle up and ride, so hang on and stay in the saddle. Trust God to show you everything you need so you can

[10] Barna, *Maximum Faith*, 22.

be led through the rivers and up the trail that continues to the glorious view of life that He has for you.

This is always a challenge for us in the church. We win people to Jesus by offering them a "free gift." We assure them that God will always be with them, and that nothing is better than living a life with Christ. I do now, and did as a full-time pastor, the same thing. If a person asked me about accepting Jesus as his or her Savior, I usually suggested that we keep it as simple as possible— sharing only the information he or she needed to know at that point in his or her faith journey. I would share with him or her the verses from Acts 2, which state that on the day of Pentecost, Peter told the people they had committed a great sin (v.36). Then the people asked Peter what they should do (v.37), to which Peter replied, "Each of you must turn from your sins and turn to God, and be baptized in the name of Jesus Christ for the forgiveness of your sins. Then you will receive the gift of the Holy Spirit" (v.38). Peter kept the answer simple; I try to do the same. Be baptized for forgiveness, which will allow you to come before God (for He cannot be around sin) and receive the free gift of the Holy Spirit, which will guide you and give you the power to live a life of following Jesus. We need to continue this in the church. Why complicate the issue of salvation? The good news in the text of Acts 2 is that some three thousand people accepted the invitation and direction from Peter. They did not question his theology, his motivation, or his instructions; they simply obeyed. This worked for Peter. Why should we handle these situations any differently?

However, this brokenness in Stop 7 of Barna's list should really be located between Stop 4 and Stop 5. We should be willing to be broken of sin at the same time we enter the church and accept salvation from the Lord, but we don't usually stress that point to new believers. Why push them away when they are just learning to walk the Christian road in life? We must win people to Christ before we can teach them to be like Christ. So when do we decide to share the good news of brokenness? Sadly, there are many people active in our churches today, who have been there for many years, who still expect easy, and still want free. These are people who still need to be fed milk, but should be challenged to move on to feasting on the meat of the gospel. There is certainly a time to set this challenge before them. As a church leader, you will need to know when that time is, and as a church member, you need to question the timing for yourself.

Mapping Brokenness

When my family took our vacation to the Rocky Mountains, we encountered many things we had never seen before. There were many new adventures, and many things to learn along the trail. In many cases, we learned on our own. In others, we stopped to ask directions, or get some clarity before we continued. Targeting transformation, on a day-to-day level, may be no different. One of the things you need to question and get clarity on is how others (and you) act, or change, when you are in this Stop of Brokenness.

George Barna is clear in his work that there are signs in the lives of people who are going through the process of Stops 6 through 10. He lists three areas that should be seen as people are advancing through these stops:

1) The *attitude shifts* that facilitate growth.
2) The *behavioral shifts* that advance maturity.
3) The *fruit* that typically emerges when a person embodies the objective of that Stop.[11]

To be specific in the area of brokenness, Barna states that we should see people begin a real shift in their *attitudes* during this

---

[11] Barna, *Maximum Faith*, 156.

stop. You will see growth in their lives that shows they are truly trusting Christ to lead them through life. The real key in this shift is to give control of your life back to God—to give God total trust, despite whatever pain or struggles may be occurring around you, or in your life. You must stay determined to let God lead in every area, and this will show the difference in attitude that others around you will see. This will be an attitude of peace and joy, while you're living in the same environment, but you are different; you're changed. As the old saying goes, "You may not be able to change your circumstances, but you can change your attitude." However, not forgetting in that statement that you are now partnering with God, and it isn't you changing your attitude by yourself.

You will also see a shift in *behavior*. People in this Stop will not be complaining about how unfair life is, or how they don't deserve the bad treatment they're receiving. Their feeling of total trust will show past their attitude and into the day-to-day behaviors. These behaviors may include an increased prayer life, or finding more time to be with God and spending less with the other distractions of modern life. People in this stop may find a renewed interest in journaling and may be able to more easily go back and read about how God has blessed them. This is also the place where finding others to help, encourage, and hold you accountable can be most helpful. This stop is not a short-term project. It takes much time and effort, but it is worth the struggle. Finding others to help, and for you to help, at this stop may be beneficial.

You also need to see *fruit*. The most noticeable sign of fruit may be humility. Humility will be developed in your life as you proceed in this process. There is something about partnering with God that humbles the proudest. When we step away from our own self-will and allow God to lead, it brings humility. You should also see a more relaxed state of being. When you learn to proceed through each day knowing that God is in control, that God has your back, and God understands the big picture of your life much better than you do, peace and relaxation become apparent.

In this phase, there is also a real understanding of God's grace. You will need to relate well to the idea that to be totally broken is to totally accept God's grace. This is a grace that completely accepts you as a sinner—saved only by His grace. When you're determined to become broken away from sin, self, and society, then your old lifestyle is replaced by a healthy understanding that you can only achieve these things because you're totally accepted by God. God is crazy in love with you, and it must bring a huge smile to His face to see you advance through this stop. Allowing yourself to see God's joy with your accomplishment is an enormous blessing that can be reached within the challenge of this stop. Your partnership with God can be most effectively realized when you completely feel and know His grace. Then your attitude, your behavior, and the fruit of your life can and will be seen freely, and given freely to others.

God has his own map and plan to guide you through brokenness, and He will not leave you during this process. In fact, He will draw closer than ever. We open the door to change and understanding, and He will lead us through that door and beyond.

CHAPTER 12
Vision of the Journey

If Jesus has divine power, he has the
supernatural ability to guide me
and help me and transform me as I follow him.
—Lee Strobel, *The Case for Christ*

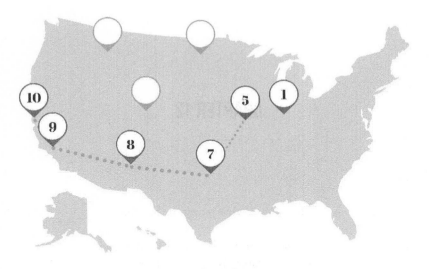

USA Map

The 10 Stops of Faith

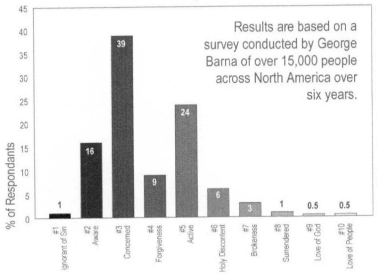

Results are based on a survey conducted by George Barna of over 15,000 people across North America over six years.

The 10 Stops of Faith

Similar to any journey we might take, in our journey of transformation, it's important to follow a good map. I thought it might be easier to explain the stops of faith by using a map you probably already know. When you look at the images on the preceding page, you'll see a map of the USA. For the purpose of this concept, pin #1 correlates with Ignorant of Sin, which is Stop 1 on the 10 Stops of Faith graph. (I introduced the idea of the 10 Stops of Faith as a map for our journey toward Christ in chapter three and described it in more detail in chapter eleven.) I have chosen to use the concept of a map as a metaphor for the stops of faith because it helps to communicate the journey—the time and the distance covered for each stop of faith.

To help illustrate the concept of using a map to show what someone's journey of transformation could look like on the ten stops of faith, we will use a fictional character—like fourteen-year-old John. Pin #1 on this map represents John's hometown in Indiana. This now becomes a faith journey map.

John has a six-year-old sister Julee. Their parents may or may not know Jesus. They may not attend any church, and they may have good reasons why. So, we as a church family, who believe in Jesus, strive to help John and Julee by providing things like vacation Bible school every summer. We also have other good programs within our church buildings. Many churches have clothing ministries, food pantries, and church outreach programs that reach deep into the communities. Many other churches have door-to-door campaigns, school mentoring opportunities, and other good and legitimate evangelistic outreach programs. If things go according to our plan, we find John and Julee and can extend a blessing to them. We reach out to them and their family with the love of Christ, we share our knowledge of Jesus, and we win these young people to Christ. We may also win the entire family, but then what?

If we fall into the familiar and normal church mode of operation, we show John and Julee around the church building, introduce them to wonderful Sunday school teachers, church leaders, and many faithful members. We also give them information on church services and ministry opportunities. In short, we connect John and Julee to the local church. In my example, this phase is represented with pin #5 on the USA Map, located at St. Louis, Missouri. This correlates with Active, Stop 5 on the 10 Stops of Faith graph. We assure John and Julee that St. Louis is a marvelous place to be, to worship, and to serve. We teach them about living the Christian life. We make sure they know that in St. Louis we have the Gateway Arch, the Cardinals, some of the best museums in the country, the beauty of the Mississippi River, and a host of other things that they will need and want. We make sure that John and Julee know the church is well located in a place that is right in the center of the country and ideally found along Interstates 70, 64, and 44 so that their family and friends can easily find their way to the good things that are happening here. In short, we sell John and Julee on the church.

Before we can do anything to help John and Julee long-term,

we must win them to Christ. Then we need to acclimate them to what the church is, why it was started, why it is here now, how it functions, how it can serve them, and how they can serve it. But then what? These souls may literally be active in the life of the church at St. Louis for the next sixty years. Good? Sure it is; but what if, someday, John or Julee want more? What if one of these—now more mature Christians—are prompted by the Holy Spirit to do more? What if one of them goes through a period of spiritual discontent and asks the church leadership for help in understanding this discontentment? Will the church suggest that this person with discontentment pray more, read the Bible more, lead a study group, or take a short-term mission trip to build their faith and overcome these discontent feelings of restlessness? These activities may all be fine, but what if there could be more? What if God has more in store for them?

What if church leadership suggests to John, for instance, who is struggling with a feeling of discontent, that maybe God is prompting him to follow the words of Paul from Romans 12:2 and be transformed by the renewing of his mind? What if church leadership set John on a path that directs him to be more like Christ, even if this decision may not, at first, seem to build up the church and meet the goals of the current church's plan of success? What if they help John by setting his sights on a journey to the beautiful city of Carmel, California? Shown with pin #10 on the USA Map, which correlates with Stop 10, Love of People on the 10 Stops of Faith graph.

If we can help John focus on this task, his life will indeed change in ways that only he and God can accomplish together. We will help John see that a partnership can be established with God that will take him through a series of stops along the road of life. His next stop could then be Tulsa, Oklahoma, shown at pin #7, which correlates with Stop 7, Brokenness.

This stop will be most challenging because it is new and different. Many people will miss their old ways and old cities. Many people come to this stop and decide it is too difficult to continue their journey to Carmel. This stop is most difficult because the sojourners are asked to partner with God's Spirit and break the idols of today. In most cases, these are idols represented by personal sin, self-pride, and the teachings of society, which are entrenched in every person's life. When this process gets too difficult, many get back on the interstate, or catch the next flight that takes them back to the safety of St. Louis. This is sad because much will be given up and abandoned; however, for those who maintain the course and overcome this stop of Brokenness, they will gain much fulfillment as they become more like Christ. They will find contentment as they continue their travels through the deserts, the mountains, and the valleys that exist in this life. Then, they may continue on their journey to Carmel.

After this stop of Brokenness, John will be free to proceed on his journey and stop at Albuquerque, New Mexico, pin #8, which correlates with Stop 8, Surrender. During this stop, John will totally surrender his life to Christ and be led only by Christ. With God's grace, he may then proceed to Bakersfield, California, pin #9, correlating with Stop 9, Love of God. This stop is where he will learn to completely love God—love as purely and as simply as God loves. Only after these stops, can John be lovingly led to Carmel.

This journey is challenging and rewarding and it may take months, years, or decades. Along the way, John and others like him will need to consult more than one map. John will need to be blessed during his travels by finding at least one loving soul (or many) who will help him. Some who can help are living in St. Louis and have already made the trip to Carmel. Some come into his life only by God's providence and blessing, but they will help in John's journey along the road of life as he makes his way to Stop 10. This is a personal journey, and John needs to travel it completely, every step of the way, in partnership with God.

What about Julee? Is she still living life and serving in St. Louis as she receives updates from her brother? Does he explain his personal challenges about the Stop of Brokenness in Tulsa? Is she encouraged by his progress as John explains the joy of reaching Stop 9 at Bakersfield? Does she marvel at how he now shares the joy of God's love from a completely new perspective? If this is new information for Julee, will she begin the journey for herself now; or, will she wait and see the magnified fruit in John's life? She will have that choice. She will make that decision.

There are also others on this journey. Many will not take the same roads that John took and many will reach their stops of faith in different "cities" on their journey. For instance, some might leave St. Louis and head north to Fargo, North Dakota to reach the Brokenness (Stop 7) part of the journey. They will stay in this area until the breaking of sin, self, and society is complete. Then, and only then, might they be led to Butte, Montana for Surrender (Stop 8). Afterward, on to Denver, Colorado, where they will learn to totally Love God, (Stop 9) before they head over the Great Divide and westward to Carmel. The path to get there is not the number one focus, the destination is—to be like Jesus.

The challenge for every individual starting this adventure is to stay the course. Focus on the goal. The goal is to reach the stage of the Christian life which Christ taught in Matthew 22:37-39, "You must love the Lord your God with all your heart, all your soul, and all your mind. This is the first and greatest commandment. A second is equally important: Love your neighbor as yourself." Love God, love people. Through this journey, John and Julee, and others like them, will learn to help other people who are also on their own journey to reach Stop 10. Each person will use whatever he or she has learned, to encourage others to be like Jesus, and to successfully complete the journey of the ten stops. That is the vision and the purpose of the targeting transformation journey.

Now, as you read the last chapter, let's begin to think about the journey as your journey. Let's make it personal.

CHAPTER 13
Make This Personal

God doesn't often reveal the details of where He's
taking you because He wants you to trust Him for
every step.
—Stormie Omartian,
Just Enough Light for the Step I'm On

I was blessed to serve in the US Army, and in 1967, I went to boot camp at Fort Campbell, Kentucky. In the first few days, the army issued me an M-14 rifle; I liked that weapon. It fit my hands well, and it felt like we'd known each other all my life. At the firing range, I found it natural to sight in my rifle, and my shooting scores were good. However, there was one man in our squad who was consistently scoring better than me. The day before our final test for marksmanship, our drill instructor, Sergeant Bailey, called out the name of the man who had the top scores. Sergeant Bailey said that, if this man earned the highest score on the range again the next day, Sergeant Bailey himself would serve the man breakfast in bed. Bailey wanted our squad to win the company wide award so he would have bragging rights over the other drill instructors in the company.

On the firing range the next day, I was focused and dead on. During the first few sets, I didn't miss. Then, on the last set, we had to move from place to place, and the targets were popping up very quickly at different locations. I saw Sergeant Bailey walk up to the scoring judge, and I heard him begin yelling and bragging to him. Because of this commotion, I lost focus on the target. I allowed a distraction to pull my attention away from my primary target. I still managed to win the marksmanship plaque, which was the highest shooting award for our basic training company, but I could have done better. I took this victory personally, and the next morning, as everyone else got up, I stayed in bed. I wondered for a few minutes if Sergeant Bailey was really going to bring me breakfast, and then reality set in. Sergeant Bailey was able to achieve bragging rights, but he had never offered to bring me breakfast, just the man he thought was going to win; so I got up and went to chow with the squad. I needed to focus on the day at hand and not on yesterday. The promise, and the marksmanship score, were never mentioned by Sergeant Bailey or myself again.

Your transformation journey is also personal, and you need to stay focused. There is no other person who can make this journey for you. There may be people along the way who can encourage you, help you, or suggest ways that will move you closer to Christ's likeness. They may even promise you a prize or reward, but you must do your part. Staying in bed will not get the job done. Focusing on some past success, or failure, will not get you through the day at hand. Expecting someone else to bring you meals, or to follow through with some outdated promise, will not help you succeed. It must be personal; it must be between you and God.

It has been my finding through the years that many people want to continue on the journey of transformation, but they stop short for a variety of reasons. Sometimes the reasons are simple. They got tired, there was drama in their life that took priority, or life just happened in a way that pulled them from the path of growth. All of these are understandable. If, or when, these things happen, you need to take care of the personal issue, and then rededicate yourself to the process. But what if things are not so understandable?

I have had the privilege of asking many people to share with me about the God they serve, or to explain to me the God they pray to. The answers are often quite revealing. These answers have taught me that there are many good Christian people who:

1) Do not know who God is,
2) are afraid of God, or
3) are a bit of both.

Many times, these people have a justified confusion of God because of some past pain in their lives that has distorted the picture of who God is in their mind. Their hearts want desperately to believe and accept a loving, caring God who loves them unconditionally, but their minds say no. This is very painful to many who choose to talk about it, and to many others the facts are just covered in darkness. They feel a need to protect that darkness, so they are unable to speak about the pain. So how can these folks say they want to be closer to God, yet they fear Him, don't understand Him, or in reality, don't want to get close to Him?

David A. Seamands, in his book *Healing of Memories*, speaks directly into the issue of our perspectives of the images of God that most often come from our childhood experiences or our parental care at different stages of life. They are something like this:

1) *The Legal God*, "keeps accounting of what we do. He waits for us to step out of line, to trip up, to falter, so He can mark us as losers."

2) *The Gotcha God*, "resembles Sherlock Holmes and wears a detective's trench coat and dark glasses. Like a disguised

126

private investigator, He is always following at a short distance. The moment we step out of line, He jumps out of the bushes and yells, 'Gotcha!' He is much like the 'corner policeman' God J.B. Phillips writes about in his excellent book, *Your God Is Too Small.*"

3) *The Sitting Bull God,* "relaxes in a yoga position on cotton candy clouds, expecting burnt offerings and homage all day long."

4) *The Philosopher's God,* "Aristotle's 'unmoved mover' of the universe, is withdrawn, cold, and distant. He is much too busy running the galaxies to get involved in our petty problems. As one man describes Him, He is silently sitting in his office, studying the encyclopedia, His door closed with a 'Do Not Disturb' sign on it."

5) *The Pharaoh God,* "is an unpleasable taskmaster who is ever increasing His demands, always upping the ante. Like Pharaoh of old, His commands move from 'Make bricks,' to 'Make more bricks,' to 'Make bricks without straw.' He is more like the horrible godfather of the mafia who always says, 'Measure up or else.'"[12]

When you carry these images, it can keep you in limbo. You are never able to advance on your spiritual journey of transformation, and therefore, you are unable to help and encourage anyone else to get one step closer to Christ. You may be focused on the past and unable to focus on the present.

I see these images of God as they relate to me when I was an eight-year-old. At that time, I saw God as a bearded old man

---

[12] David Seamands, *Healing of Memories* (Wheaton: SP Publications, 1986), 104–5.

standing above me, sternly pointing his finger at me in displeasure. In some ways that image took the place of my strong and stern grandmother, who had passed away. It took many years of self-examination, prayer, and study to get past that image and accept God's grace into my life. To concede, and then to truly believe that God could love a sinful person like me, was not just a huge step of faith but a leap of trust as well. It was monumental.

Basically, what if your only focus is to look at every person you meet as a soul needing to get closer to God? What if you didn't see color, ethnicity, or sexual orientation? What if you see yourself as one who is totally loved by the God who is the Creator, Savior, and Counselor—and then take that same image and allow it to be used and given to every person you meet, every day of your life? That is targeting transformation at its finest! You will be blessed by this process, you will grow closer to God in doing it, and you will bless the people you encounter every day.

Seeing an image of God's loving hands, open to accept you as His child, can become the turning point in the process of transformation for your life and can compel you to actually target transformation with every person you meet in your life.

It would be my hope that you can learn to accept God as Jesus describes Him in the parable of the lost son (Luke 15:11–24). In this text, Jesus labors to share the concept of God as the loving father who is always looking for his lost son, and when the father's eyes see his son returning home, he runs to hug him. No greeting could be sweeter, no reunion more illustrative of grace. The son needn't speak, for his father loves the son so much that he wants to throw a party to welcome him home. The father has no stern words of condemnation, no long list of sins or impending punishment to pay for the son's departure. The father is simply extending grace with no end or measure. That's the view of God that Jesus describes, and when you keep that image in mind, it is humbling and life-changing. Not only will the acceptance of this transform your life, but it will allow you to share that same image with every person you meet, every single day.

Without this image, it is easy to become judgmental of the people you meet. It's easy to not see the pain, or the need. It's easy to live your life in the bubble of self, and forget about the love of Christ that you need to share. When this image of a loving God, extending His grace, is allowed to surround your heart, then you will be able to share that love with others. In fact, you won't be able to keep from sharing it. That, my friends, is when targeting transformation works. Go for it! Join the challenge of targeting transformation, and live it day-to-day. Make it personal!

APPENDIX
Taking the Targeting
Transformation Challenge

Church Challenge

The targeting transformation challenge is simple: Let's have churches join together to change the culture of their communities. We ask that you do three things:

1. *Pray* for people to have the courage and desire to continue their journey of transformation and helping others do the same.
2. *Pledge* to prepare sermons with the purpose of transformation in mind, and then be clear about your purpose with a statement like, "This message is designed to help you in your transformation journey."
3. Begin to *encourage and train* your staff and your congregation to use the LOVE system in their day-to-day, person-to-person encounters.

Personal Challenge

You can personally pledge to:
1. Totally commit yourself to your own transformation growth.
2. Pledge to implement the targeting transformation ideals for people in your life by using the LOVE system each day.

Then, enjoy the progress of your own transformation growth, and take joy in seeing other people change and move forward in their personal journey to become like Jesus.

Connect with Our Community
Sign-up for encouragement and updates at <u>www.targetingtransformation.com</u>.
Like us on Facebook.

Thank you,
Ray D. Ellis and the Targeting Transformation Team

BIBLIOGRAPHY

Barna, George. *Maximum Faith: Live Like Jesus*. Austin: Fedd and Company, 2011.

Cloud, Henry. *Necessary Endings*. New York: HarperCollins, 2010.

Cottrell, Jack. *The College Press NIV Commentary: Romans*. Vol. 2. Joplin: College Press Publishing Company, 1998.

Cowman, Mrs. Charles E. *Streams in the Desert: A Daily Devotional Journal*. Uhrichsville: Barbour Publishing, Inc., 1965.

Cymbala, Jim. *Fresh Wind, Fresh Fire*. Grand Rapids: Zondervan, 1997.

Ellis, Joe S. *The Church on Purpose: Keys to Effective Church Leadership*. Cincinnati: Standard Publishing, 1982.

Faust, David. *Taking Truth Next Door*. Cincinnati: Standard Publishing, 1999.

Guinness, Os, and John Seel. *No God but God*. Chicago: Moody Press, 1992.

Hybels, Bill. *Too Busy Not to Pray*. Downers Grove: InterVarsity Press, 2008.

Ogden, Greg. *Transforming Discipleship*. Downers Grove: InterVarsity Press, 2003.

Seamands, David A. *Healing of Memories*. Wheaton: SP Publications, 1986.